The
University
of
Wisconsin

A Pictorial History

Arthur Hove   with the editorial assistance of Anne Biebel

THE UNIVERSITY OF
WISCONSIN
A PICTORIAL HISTORY

THE UNIVERSITY OF WISCONSIN PRESS

The University of
Wisconsin Press
114 North Murray Street
Madison, Wisconsin 53715

3 Henrietta Street
London WC2E 8LU, England

Printed in the
United States of America

Library of Congress Cataloging-in-Publication Data

Hove, Arthur.
    The University of Wisconsin: a pictorial history / by Arthur Hove with
with the editorial assistance of Anne Biebel.
    366 pp.   cm.
    Includes bibliographical references (pp. 339–341) and index.
    1. University of Wisconsin—Madison—History.   2. University of
Wisconsin—Madison—Description—Views.   I. Biebel, Anne.
II. Title.
LD6128H68   1991
378.775'83—dc20   90-26466
ISBN 0-299-13000-2   CIP

This book is dedicated

to the memory of

PETER BUNN

(1930–1983)

Secretary of the Faculty,

1978–1983

Contents

Preface

This book complements the many histories and accounts that deal with the continuing and complex evolution of the University of Wisconsin. Wherever possible, the stereotypical has been avoided or minimized. Images have been selected to give the distinctive feel of the respective historical periods and to reveal the qualities of the individuals who have shaped the university. The images eloquently testify to their collective achievement.

Obviously, no single volume can cover every aspect of such a complex institution. Nor can it anticipate the special interests of various constituencies and readers. Apologies are due to those who feel that something is missing from this portfolio. The omissions are not intentional; they merely reflect the fact that the record of a great institution is never complete. There is always more to be done, more to uncover.

Acknowledgments

The impetus for this volume emerged from discussions among University of Wisconsin Press staff in 1983. At that time, the newly appointed director of the press, Allen Fitchen, and his colleagues Ezra S. Diman, associate director, and Peter Givler, general editor, felt there was a logical need for a book to complement the exemplary Curti and Carstensen two-volume history which had been published in conjunction with the university's centennial.

Chancellor Irving Shain gave his unqualified support to the project following review and endorsement by Graduate School dean Robert M. Bock, associate deans Edwin Black, David Ward, and Mareda Weiss, and Letters and Science dean E. David Cronon. An advisory committee subsequently drafted a proposal which addressed, among other matters, editorial principles, purposes of publication, and the intended audience for the book. The committee consisted of Fitchen, Diman, J. Frank Cook, university archivist, Edward M. Coffman, professor of history, and myself. Special recognition must go to Dean Cronon, whose early enthusiasm for the project was accompanied by many useful suggestions about historical methodology and whose knowledge of the university proved to be a continuing source of insight and perspective. Chancellor Donna E. Shalala, who succeeded Irving Shain following his retirement, has continually reinforced the idea that a university must be imbued with a clear sense of history and tradition.

A grant from the Brittingham Fund helped get the project under way. Ronald Weber, as project assistant, made the initial forays into pertinent photo and document collections to confirm that an extensive and rich body of material was available. He was succeeded by Anne Biebel, whose uncommon level of support and involvement earned the recognition reflected in the credit on the title page.

In a project as large and complex as this one, compiling and editing relevant material involved the talents, resources, and services of a large number of people and institutions. The following primary sources were searched and utilized for appropriate documentary evidence, photos, and graphic material: University of Wisconsin–Madison Archives; Iconography Division, State Historical Society of Wisconsin; Photographic Media Center, University Extension; University of Wisconsin–Madison News Service; and the Madison *Capital Times*, the *Wisconsin State Journal*, the *Daily Cardinal*, and the *Milwaukee Journal*.

A number of alumni, faculty, staff, and friends shared their photo and memorabilia collections and their personal remembrances at various points during the development of the project. Their enthusiasm for the university provided a continuing source of encouragement. Prominent among this group were Ira Baldwin, professor emeritus of bacteriology and vice president for academic affairs under E. B. Fred, and Porter Butts, director of the Memorial Union for nearly four decades.

The staff of the University Archives was unflaggingly cooperative. In addition to J. Frank Cook, Bernard Schermetzler was enormously patient and helpful in finding the appropriate images and tracking down crucial points of fact. James Liebig, who managed the archives collection housed in the Steenbock Library, also was consistently helpful, as was Barry Teicher, head of the oral history project. The staff of the Iconography Division of the State Historical Society—George Talbot, Myrna Williamson, and Christine Schelshorn—helped supplement material not found in university collections. John O. Holzhueter of the State Historical Society provided contextual information, especially as it related to state history, along with a heavy dose of moral support. Others who cooperated in this vein were Jack Lund, Gary Schulz, and Duane Hopp of the University Extension Photographic Media Center; Thomas H. Murphy, former editor of the *Wisconsin Alumnus*; and Michael Kienitz, of the University News Service, whose photographs form the majority of the collection reproduced in the color portfolio.

Several individuals read the manuscript in its numerous versions and offered helpful and often trenchant comments and suggestions. These include the members of the original editorial committee; Dean Cronon; Bernard C. Cohen, emeritus professor of political science and former vice chancellor for academic affairs and acting chancellor; Phillip R. Certain, professor of chemistry and former associate vice chancellor for academic affairs; Patricia C. Anderson, executive director of the Wisconsin Humanities

Committee; James S. Watrous, professor emeritus of art history; and John W. Jenkins of the University History Project. Jenkins corroborated points of fact and reminded the author that the active voice is better than the passive.

Jim Watrous, whose personal remembrances and knowledge of the university added an important perspective, graciously provided working and storage space at the beginning of the project. This proved invaluable in the assembling of the early drafts of the manuscript and its accompanying illustrations. Elizabeth Steinberg, Raphael Kadushin, Carol Olsen, and Gardner Wills, of the University of Wisconsin Press, shepherded the manuscript through the publication process; Angela Ray brought order and style to the manuscript as copy editor; and designer Rich Hendel transformed the material into a visually exciting format.

I further benefited from the wisdom and observations of countless individuals from my student days, which began in the fall of 1952, to the present. I was fortunate to have had numerous talks with E. B. Fred, whose knowledge of the university and dedication to its principles were inspiring. I also am grateful to those heads of the university who have given me the opportunity to pursue my professional career in response to their leadership: Fred Harvey Harrington, Edwin Young, Glenn Pound, Irving Shain, Bernard C. Cohen, and Donna E. Shalala.

Robert Taylor, Fannie Taylor, Bryant Kearl, Joseph C. Corry, Joel Skornicka, Len Van Ess, Clay Schoenfeld, Ted Crabb, Harry Peterson, and Robert W. Brennan have also provided help. Colleagues in my immediate professional area—Arlie M. Mucks, Jr., Gayle Langer, Robert B. Rennebohm, John F. Newman, Linda Weimer, Albert C. Friedman, John Gruber, and Earl Madden—have contributed their assistance and support through the years. Still others, too numerous to single out for specific mention, have touched my life at the university and given me a deep appreciation for its breadth, depth, and diversity.

My wife, Norma, and our sons, Jim, Bill, and Tom, have given me the human sustenance and reinforcement that cannot be adequately quantified or reciprocated.

This book is formally dedicated to a friend and colleague who personified the fact that great institutions derive their identity, strength, and character from those who lend their talents and personal qualities to the search for an ideal. This distinctive spirit has been apparent at the University of Wisconsin throughout its history.

The
University
of
Wisconsin

A Pictorial History

Prologue | Before the Settlers Came

At first Wisconsin was the bed of a prehistoric sea. The sea receded, and the scraping and gouging of a series of glaciers made over the land. When the last ice sheet retreated, it left a countryside of rolling hills and crystal-clear lakes. The lakes and the rich soil encouraged the growth of plant and animal life. Humans first appeared in the area about twelve thousand years ago. A strong local culture developed approximately a millennium ago. The people of the time left substantial evidence of their presence in the form of effigy mounds, patterns of raised earth shaped like animals—birds, turtles, bears, beaver. In recent times, Woodland Indians inhabited the area—the Menominee, Potawatomi, Winnebago, and Chippewa. They hunted, fished, and lived off the providence of the land. They gave the area a name, Taychopera, the Winnebago name for the area's four lakes.

Then the first wave of settlers came, displacing the Indians. The new people came predominantly from New England, from another world, another culture. They moved into an area which had been politically outlined by the Northwest Ordinance of 1787. The territory eventually became the states of Ohio, Michigan, Indiana, Illinois, and Wisconsin. A prime mover in the adoption of this ordinance, originally drafted by Thomas Jefferson, was Nathan Dane, who was subsequently memorialized in the name of the county which would contain the site of the University of Wisconsin. The ordinance, in typical Jeffersonian language, established a climate for education by noting: "Religion, morality, and knowledge, being necessary to good government and the happiness of mankind, schools and the means of education shall forever be encouraged [in the territory]."

As the incursions by settlers from the East began, the Native Americans were gradually displaced. An early and dramatic episode in Wisconsin history highlights the efforts to secure the frontier for development. On July 21, 1832, a combination of army regulars and militia, commanded by General Henry Atkinson, pursued the Fox-Sauk Indian chief Black Hawk and a band of his followers through a portion of what later became the University of Wisconsin campus. The following day a skirmish occurred at Wisconsin Heights, a few miles northwest of Madison. Black Hawk and his people were overwhelmed and forced to move westward.

The frontier had arrived.

Before white settlers from the East moved into the area, the land that now is the campus served as a focus for various waves of Native American *settlement. Cultural artifacts from the pre-Columbian period include the effigy mounds found on Observatory Hill and near the base of Picnic Point. The* *huge Chamberlin Boulder on the hill is a graphic reminder of the Wisconsin glacier which covered the land more than ten thousand years ago.*

ACTIVITIES

Woodland Indians, the most recent native settlers in the Four Lakes region, named many of the area's landmarks and created a body of lore and legend which has become a part of the local heritage. This illustration from the 1928 Badger yearbook is an idealized depiction of an aspect of their culture.

This marker, placed next to the Carillon Tower on Bascom Hill, commemorates a significant moment in Wisconsin history. Black Hawk and his warriors retreated through the area; they were later cornered and suffered heavy casualties at the junction of the Bad Axe River and the Mississippi.

From
College
to
University

The leaders who developed the Wisconsin frontier and its outposts showed an early interest in providing for the establishment of a university. The First Territorial Assembly of Wisconsin, meeting in 1836, authorized the sale of land to generate funds for "an academy for the education of youth." The Congress of the United States shortly thereafter made a similar authorization for a "Seminary of Learning in the Territory of Wisconsin." The Wisconsin Constitution, adopted in 1848, specifically provided "for the establishment of a State University, at or near the seat of state government." It also decreed that "no sectarian instruction shall be allowed in such university."

Wisconsin achieved statehood on May 29, 1848. In the summer of that year, the legislature established the university and directed that it should be governed by a board of regents and administered by a chancellor. By October the regents had met, authorized expenditures (as yet unfunded), and established a curriculum consisting primarily of ancient and modern geography, English grammar, and Latin and Greek. They also made their first appointments. University of Missouri president John H. Lathrop was named chancellor at an annual salary of two thousand dollars, and John W. Sterling was appointed professor and head of the preparatory department at a salary of five hundred dollars a year.

The idea of a university had become a reality, even though its translation from plan to program was still primitive. "It is well remarked," commented the Madison *Argus and Democrat* on February 6, 1849, "that the University will occupy the highest place in our educational system; that from its design it must necessarily embrace a wide range of study, and a severe course of mental discipline." That severe course was quite evident in the early days. The learning was classical, and the living was spartan.

The early students came from varied educational backgrounds, and few had completed what we now regard as a systematic college preparatory program. Students were expected to buy their own food, furniture, and straw to fill their mattresses. The school year consisted of three terms of thirteen weeks each. Tuition and the cost of a room for the year in 1853 was twenty-four dollars. The first degrees granted by the university were awarded in 1854 to Levi Booth and Charles T. Wakeley. Seven years later, in 1861, there were enough graduates on the rolls to precipitate the founding of the Wisconsin Alumni Association.

Although the state constitution provided that "no sectarian instruction shall be allowed," daily attendance at chapel was compulsory in the early days. When they were not studying or worshiping, students found a number of sources for diversion. The scenic campus and the bountiful surroundings made boating, hunting, fishing, and foraging for food popular activities. Playing quoits, wickets, and sometimes baseball provided physical recreation. Intellectual interests were centered on literary publications such as the *Students' Miscellany*. Professor Sterling organized the first literary society, the Athenaean, in 1850.

The aspirations of the university's founders were high, but at the same time they had a fundamentally democratic orientation. Chancellor Lathrop held that public universities should serve the public. The catalog for 1853 indicated: "It is the fixed intention of the university authorities, that all the means at their command shall be so administered as to aid the diligent and successful student, and to secure to the institution a just public confidence and support."

The proper means to achieve that goal has been a matter of discussion and periodic contention throughout the history of the university. Before the nineteenth century, only those of the ruling or economically advanced class commonly had access to advanced learning. Higher learning promoted the refinement of the mind and stimulated the cultivation of aesthetic and moral sensibilities. The curriculum dealt with the great writers and thinkers of the past who were considered the primary sources of wisdom and perception. Such an attitude, however, did not necessarily conform to life on the frontier, a place where the most important concern was coping with realities found in the often raw, untamed wilderness. Early catalogs of the university stress instruction in the "useful arts" and "industrial pursuits."

In 1862 the United States Congress passed the Morrill Act, which provided lands to be sold to create endowments. The resulting land-grant colleges and universities were to offer, among other subjects, instruction in the agricultural and mechanical arts. In speaking of the agricultural program in the College of Arts at Wisconsin, the university catalog for 1868 said the department offered "a thorough course of instruction directly pertaining to Agriculture which will enable [the graduates of the program] to conduct the operations of a farm both intelligently and profitably."

Nevertheless, a considerable portion of the early curriculum had a classical orientation. It emphasized algebra, geometry, trigonometry, calculus, and a study of classical Greek and Roman authors. There also were courses on mechanics, physics, botany, and chemistry, as well as ethics, philosophy, and civil polity.

Initially, the legislature had authorized the sale of public lands to endow the university. Unfortunately, the lands were sold at a price low enough to encourage settlement of the state, but too low to produce sufficient funds for development or to build an endowment. By the 1860s it had become obvious that the university's expenses were exceeding its means. While the sale of lands granted by the federal government through the Morrill Act provided some relief, it was not enough. In 1867 the legislature authorized a one-time appropriation to help the regents retire accrued indebtedness. The legislature further responded to the university's fiscal problems in 1870 by granting a one-time appropriation of fifty thousand dollars. Two years later the legislature passed a bill ensuring a ten-thousand-dollar annual appropriation. In 1876 the legislature granted the university one-tenth of a mill for every dollar of assessed value on all property in the state. This rate was increased to one-eighth of a mill in 1882.

A dramatic event in 1884 led to further legislative support. Fire gutted the original Science Hall and destroyed many art treasures, valuable museum pieces, and scientific apparatuses. The legislature moved promptly to provide funds to replace the structure and its contents, underscoring the increasing importance of the university to the state.

Meanwhile, the problem of leadership and administrative continuity led to restructuring. In 1866 the legislature reorganized the university, primarily to change the method for selecting regents. The regents, originally elected by the legislature, were now to be appointed by the governor on the basis of geographical considerations. Two would come from each of the state's congressional districts, and three would be chosen at large. There were to be additional appointments of ex-officio state constitutional officers. Regent bylaws subsequently gave specific powers to the regents for controlling university affairs, including the annual election of the president (previously chancellor) and the appointment of the faculty.

As the university matured, gaining additional faculty and students, the curriculum shifted away from the classical subjects, and students were allowed more flexibility in choosing their courses of study. Professor J. F. A. Pyre, in his 1920 history of the university, noted that by the beginning of the 1880s, during John Bascom's administration, "the Greek course began to fall away, not only in relative, but in absolute numbers. . . . the set was increasingly toward modern subjects, toward science, and toward the technical departments."

While it is difficult to describe the typical student of the time, a history of the graduating class of 1874 written by Kate McGonegal and John Brindley does offer an interesting profile of the class. The class included twenty-six men and fourteen women, the largest number to graduate up to that point. The authors noted that "10 are wholly and 5 are partially self-supporting. The largest annual expenses of any one member is $400, smallest is $200, average is $295. 1 will study for the ministry, 2 will be civil engineers. Three will make teaching their occupation and 13 will soar to fame or hover about starvation in the profession of law."

No record exists of the number of students who either soared or hovered from those early days. Most, we can presume, entered society and lived useful and constructive lives following their university experience. Occasionally, one would become the stuff of legend—such as John Muir, Robert M. La Follette, and Charles R. Van Hise.

The men elected to lead the university through its formative years experienced varying degrees of success. John H. Lathrop was the first in a series of leaders who touched the university but did not impress it with an indelible stamp. A man of considerable education and impressive appearance, Lathrop had studied at Hamilton College in New York and at Yale University, and he demonstrated eloquence in his writing and public speaking. He emphasized the importance of education, particularly as the natural extension of a democratic society. Throughout his administration, he stressed the need to establish a unified public education system extending from elementary school to the university. His relations with the regents and students were cordial and often influential, but the faculty did not hold a similar esteem for him. Some thought him "dictatorial and autocratic" and out of touch with recent developments in higher education.

Lathrop stayed ten years, leaving in 1859 to become president of Indiana University. His successor, Henry Barnard, had a national reputation that placed him on a par with Horace Mann, the noted educator and public reformer. Barnard's stay, however, was brief and punctuated by periods of illness which left him little time or energy to move the university forward. He resigned in 1861.

As the regents searched for a new president, they called on the ever-dependable John Sterling to take Barnard's place. Sterling served as acting president throughout the Civil War period. He did everything from selling used furniture to students to keeping the university records and looking after the buildings and grounds. At the same time he administered university affairs and taught classes in mathematics and other subjects. Although he appealed periodically for relief from his many assignments, the regents did not respond. They took advantage of his loyalty and broad skills, and he dutifully continued to provide stability and continuity in an uncertain time.

Sterling served until 1867, when the regents selected Paul A. Chadbourne, professor of sciences at Williams College, as the new president. Although his stay in Wisconsin was relatively brief (he resigned in 1870 to accept the Williams College presidency), he established an effective relationship with the faculty and the regents. Chadbourne proved to be a skillful administrator who provided the groundwork for the important growth and development that emerged during the Bascom administration.

The next president proved less adroit. John H. Twombly, a Methodist minister in Charleston, Massachusetts, was elected to the presidency on June 30, 1871, primarily at the urging of Samuel Fallows, a member of the UW class of 1859, who was bishop of the local Reformed Episcopal Church. While he was an effective speaker and an outspoken advocate of coeducation, Twombly nevertheless alienated the regents, who soon sought his removal. Even though he managed to gain support from the public, the students, and the legislature, Twombly resigned when it became obvious that the regents were determined to maintain control over the university.

John Bascom succeeded Twombly in 1874. Like Chadbourne, he had an association with Williams College. A man of considerable intellect and forceful will, Bascom had a distinguished record as a scholar, demonstrating proficiency in such fields as mathematics, theology, psychology, English literature, aesthetics, and political economy. He also was committed to such issues as women's rights (and consequently coeducation) and social and economic justice. In addition, he advocated temperance and supported labor unions and the right to strike.

Bascom brought his full concentration to the presidency, serving as both a moral leader and an effective administrator. He believed that the individual had a responsibility to become involved in the moral issues of the day. His views were nurtured during successive administrations and came to a dramatic and full flowering as the Wisconsin Idea, a program of public service advanced by President Charles R. Van Hise and Governor Robert M. La Follette, both former students of Bascom's.

Bascom felt strongly that the regents should remove themselves from the day-to-day activities of the university. Their task, as he viewed it, was to avoid meddling in educational matters and to secure the resources that would allow the faculty to realize their "educational objectives."

Not all the regents were persuaded, most prominently Elisha W. ("Boss") Keyes. Chairman of the executive committee and a judge, Keyes also served as Madison mayor and postmaster and chairman of the state Republican party. Because Bascom strongly advocated prohibition and called for diminished influence of the regents in the university's everyday administration, it was obvious that the two would be antagonists. Keyes had numerous and sometimes questionable business interests, including the sale of liquor in the community. The struggle between the two smoldered and sometimes flared through most of the 1880s.

Eventually Bascom acknowledged that his effectiveness as president would be continually compromised as long as he had irreconcilable differences with the regents. In late 1885 he indicated that he might offer his resignation the following June, to become effective a year later. The regents chose to interpret this as a formal resignation rather than a statement of intent. They moved rapidly to seek a successor, turning to Thomas Chrowder Chamberlin, an official with the United States Geological Survey. Chamberlin accepted the presidency in the late spring of 1886 but indicated that he could not come until the following year because of previous professional commitments.

The changing guard denoted the university's arrival at a significant demarcation point. Although his administration had been punctuated with controversy, John Bascom had stimulated the transformation of the institution into a college of growing stature. He had done so by his personal example and by insisting on academic excellence. Even though he was often distant from his faculty, he nurtured and fought for faculty governance, a principle which enhanced academic quality as it gained prominence in later years.

This map shows the location and proposed development of the university campus, originally known as College Hill. The initial campus tract of 157.5 acres was purchased from Aaron Vanderpool of New York City at a cost of fifteen dollars per acre, plus taxes for the current year and a 2½ percent commission for the real estate agents. Many of the platted streets have disappeared or had their names changed, but the major elements of the plan remain, including the railroad tracks bisecting the campus.

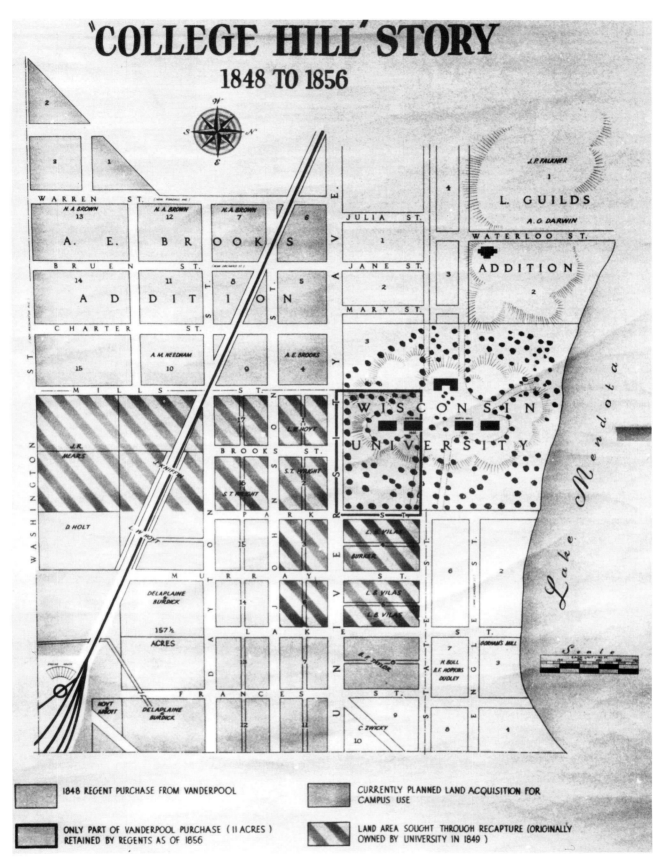

"COLLEGE HILL" STORY
1848 TO 1856

1848 REGENT PURCHASE FROM VANDERPOOL

ONLY PART OF VANDERPOOL PURCHASE (11 ACRES) RETAINED BY REGENTS AS OF 1856

CURRENTLY PLANNED LAND ACQUISITION FOR CAMPUS USE

LAND AREA SOUGHT THROUGH RECAPTURE (ORIGINALLY OWNED BY UNIVERSITY IN 1849)

Professor John W. Sterling met the first class, consisting of seventeen boys from Madison and the surrounding area, in a rent-free room of the Madison Female Academy (pictured here) on February 5, 1849.

The Female Academy (the low building with the rectangular white roof at left of center in this photograph from the 1860s) stood north of City Hall at the corner of Dayton Street and Wisconsin Avenue. This location subsequently served as the site of Madison High School, also called Madison Central High School and Central University High. In 1969 it became the campus of the Madison Area Technical College. Picnic Point, minus much of its now-familiar vegetation, appears in the distance.

John F. Rague set forward the first plan for development of College Hill. This illustration, taken from the September 6, 1851, issue of Gleason's Pictorial, *shows the university's first three buildings (South Hall, University Hall, and North Hall) flanked by two additional dormitories that were never built. The capstone of the hill, University Hall, was completed in 1859. The plans for the building were executed by the Irish-American architect William Tinsley, who worked out of Indianapolis, Indiana. There seems to be no functional rationale for the building's Italian High Renaissance style. The regents apparently just instructed Tinsley to follow Rague's plan and develop a domed structure.*

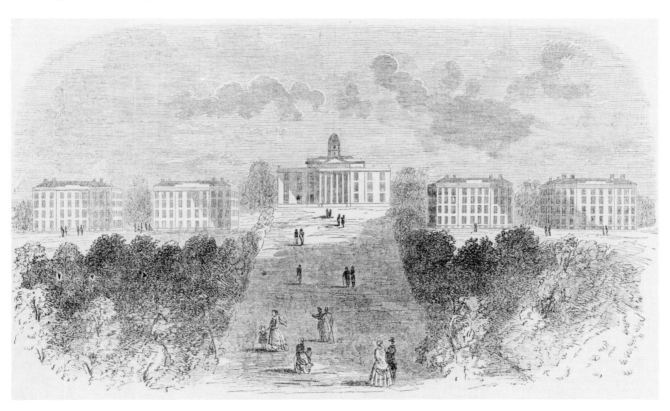

By 1859 the three main buildings of the university had been constructed and presented an impressive and imposing aspect on College Hill.

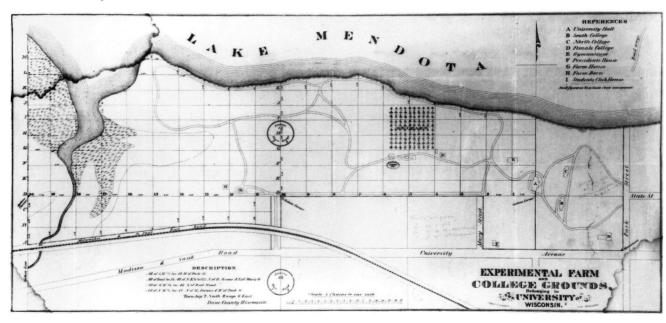

This 1875 section map illustrates the expansion of the campus. The original forty-acre tract expanded to 235 acres in 1866, when additional land was purchased for development of the experimental farm. The map also shows that consideration was being given at the time to the placement of additional campus facilities and the flow of traffic through the area.

John Hiram Lathrop, the university's first chancellor, assumed his duties in the fall of 1849 after relinquishing his previous position as president of the University of Missouri. Eloquent in his speeches and written statements, Lathrop proved to be more a man of words than of deeds. University historians Merle Curti and Vernon Carstensen observed that "his coming was greeted with delight; his resignation ten years later was accepted without reluctance."

Simeon Mills, a Madison businessman, legislative leader, and public servant, introduced the legislation which became the first charter of the university. Mills served as a regent from 1848 to 1853 and was instrumental in the purchase of the university campus and in superintending construction of the first building.

Eleazer Root, the state's first superintendent of public instruction, is credited with framing the article in the state constitution which established the University of Wisconsin.

Hiram Smith, a leading agriculturalist, dairy farmer, and founder and president of the Wisconsin Dairyman's Association, served as a regent from 1878 to 1890. He helped establish the first dairy school in the United States at the university and promoted development of the College of Agriculture. He is remembered today through Hiram Smith Hall, part of the initial cluster of buildings that formed the agricultural campus.

COMMENCEMENT
Of the State University.

July 26th, 1854.

SCHEME.

MUSIC.

PRAYER.

MUSIC.

SALUTATORY - - Addresses, in Latin. - - - LEVI BOOTH,
ORATION - - The Eastern Question. - - - - JAMES M. FLOWER.
    Nature, Man's best Teacher. - - - SIDNEY FOOTE.

MUSIC.

ORATION. - - The Ideal Man, - - - - - - H. K. SMITH.
    The Legal Profession. - - - - JAMES HICKOX.

MUSIC.

ORATION. - - Imperfections of the Social System. - LEVI BOOTH.
    The Course of Liberal Study : with the
    VALEDICTORY ADDRESSES.   CHAS. T. WAKELEY.

MUSIC.

Degrees Conferred.

MUSIC.

BACCALAUREATE ADDRESS, by the Chancellor.

MUSIC.

BENEDICTION.

Contrary to the reservations of the Madison Argus and Democrat *editor, Levi Booth managed to lead a productive life. After receiving his baccalaureate, he completed a master's degree and moved to Colorado, where he became a successful rancher and held several public offices.*

The first commencement ceremony set a pattern for subsequent generations of students. The program featured considerable speaking punctuated by music. The university's first two graduates, of those who had assembled in 1849 as the first class, were Levi Booth and Charles T. Wakeley. The editor of the Madison Argus and Democrat *observed that Wakeley had "not much been injured by his scholastic acquirements and associations" but Booth had "much good sense yet to acquire to make his college learning of any avail to himself."*

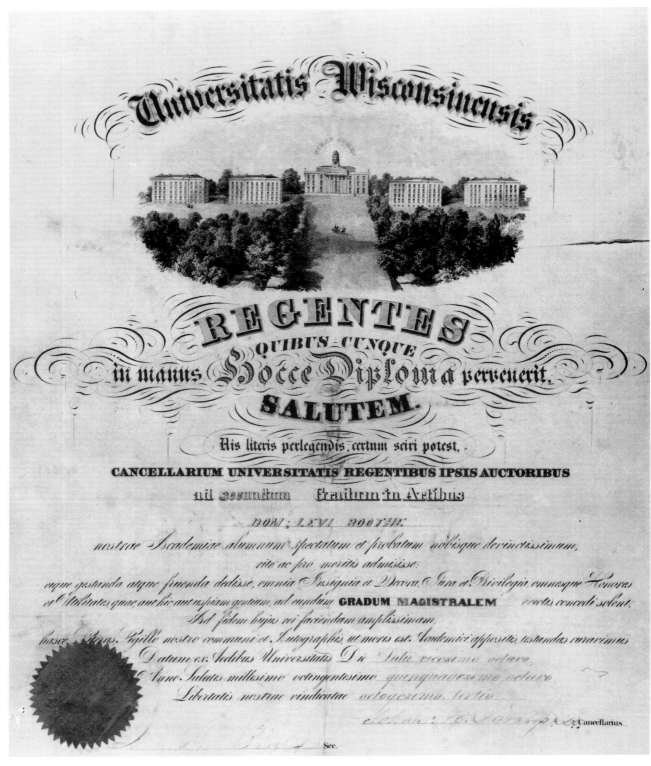

*Booth's 1858 master's diploma
is the earliest surviving example
of an official university
diploma.*

THE

STUDENTS'

Miscellany.

CONDUCTED BY

MEMBERS OF THE ATHENÆAN SOCIETY,

OF THE

WISCONSIN STATE UNIVERSITY.

"HÆC STUDIA ADOLESCENTIAM ALUNT."

MADISON, WIS.:
ATWOOD & RUBLEE, PRINTERS.
BRUEN'S BLOCK.

Vol. I.]   JANUARY, 1857.   [No. 1.

When the Students' Miscellany first appeared in *1857*, the editor noted the reason for its publication, claiming that "no society, business firm, or literary institution can acquire or maintain its appropriate position before the public, without making use of the ordinary means of advertising."

John W. Sterling was a faculty member for thirty-seven years, spanning the administrations from Lathrop to Bascom. A stabilizing influence through the various periods of early development, he served as acting president from 1861 to 1867. When he died at age sixty-nine in 1885, his picture was displayed at the funeral service along with a large banner bearing the motto "Father of the University— 1848–1885." He is seen here in his familiar role, as pater-familias, with his own family: wife, Harriet; daughters, Grace and Susan; and son, Charles.

*The earliest available photo of
a university graduating class is
this portrait of the class of 1861.
Front row: William E. Spencer,
James B. Britton, Jr., Shadrach
Hall, John D. Parkinson, and
Almerin Gillett. Back row:
William W. Church, Henry
Vilas, Farlin Q. Ball, and
Michael A. Leahy.*

This illustration from the November 20, 1858, issue of Frank Leslie's Illustrated Weekly *shows North and South halls framing the familiar view up State Street to the capitol.* The university was then situated on the outskirts of town.

Throughout the Civil War, Camp Randall served as an important training ground for Wisconsin troops and as a hospital and a Confederate prison. It ultimately became the site of the university's engineering campus and the major portion of the intercollegiate athletic facilities. University Heights appears in the center background of this 1864 illustration. The railroad tracks which lead toward Prairie du Chien still bisect the campus at University Avenue. The road at the left, the present-day Regent Street, linked Madison and Mineral Point. The camp, named after Governor Alexander Randall (1858–1862), subsequently became the State Fair Grounds. The university purchased the property in 1893 for an athletic field.

John Muir, one of the students from the early period, distinguished himself after leaving the university in 1863. He lived in North Hall and was noted for his inventive mind and facility for constructing labor-saving gadgets. The elaborate clock pictured here moved books up and down for study according to a set routine. During his career as a naturalist, Muir fought to preserve the California redwoods and helped establish the Sierra Club. He is regarded as the father of the National Park System.

Henry Barnard succeeded Lathrop as chancellor of the university in 1859 following a complete reorganization by the regents. Although he was a nationally recognized educator, his periodic illnesses and absence from the campus made him a largely ineffective leader.

By the time Paul A. Chadbourne became head of the university, the title of the chief executive had been changed from chancellor to president. Chadbourne stimulated important changes during his administration (1867–1870), including an expansion of the academic program and the appointment of new faculty. He also managed to secure a fifty-thousand-dollar appropriation from the legislature to construct the university's fourth building, which would serve as a separate Female College. The separate building reflected Chadbourne's feeling that women should not be admitted to equal status with men.

Completed in 1871, Ladies Hall originally housed the Female College, but it became solely a women's dormitory after women were fully integrated into the academic program following Chadbourne's departure. The original structure remained in use until 1959, when it was removed to make way for a new eleven-story women's dormitory constructed on the same site. The original building received *the ironic designation of Chadbourne Hall in the early 1920s, when President Edward A. Birge selected the name to call attention to Chadbourne's opposition to coeducation.*

John H. Twombly, the university's fourth president, served from 1871 to 1874. The regents hired the Methodist minister with the hope that he would be an effective fund-raiser, but Twombly did not fulfill the expectations. He never managed to gain the confidence and support of the faculty, and he left behind only his strong advocacy for the education of women.

John Bascom, who served from 1874 to 1887, transformed the university from a somewhat glorified preparatory school into a college of solid academic stature. Bascom's strong sense of morality and his dedication to learning set an example for faculty and students. An advocate for public higher education, Bascom believed that the state had the duty to provide educational opportunities for its citizens. He is shown here after he left the university and returned to New England.

This student broadside from 1873 gives an idea of the type of topical humor popular at the time. Obviously, nothing is sacred, and no one is immune from satiric treatment.

This late 1870s view of Observatory Hill with Washburn Observatory and a small solar observatory at left and University Hall in the background reveals the westward expansion of the campus as the university increased in size and complexity.

MOGUL and STAFF.

Big Mogul and Nose Wiper—J(EHUDA) H(ANNASI) TWOMBLY—will have charge of the snotty Seniors to whom he will administer soothing syrup at frequent intervals. He was once Principal of a Grammar School on the outskirts of Boston but was kicked out on account of ignorance and extreme boorishness. As President of the University (run by Pat and the Frishmen) he exercises about as much authority as pink eyed Billy does over the ass. Legislature. He presides in the class in Theology taught by Bash and Hutch. When the belching and snivelling has ceased, Prex will give each senior a complimentary ticket to the Grand Drama "Peter Arden" played to-night at the Lake Shore House by Faculty and Regents, (Prex as Pete.)

J(ANE) STERLING. This *damsel* has been trying to pass himself off for a Prof. If the small boys will keep still he will be seen coming on the stage with his head up and tail rising, at the same time blowing his old bugle. He will then go to the board and demonstrate by Jonl's law just how much wine he, Schmitz and Brekheimer drank at Baraboo on the Methodist Excursion. He will then state that he is a very great sinner, but is willing to be forgiven. His room is at No. 10; any one coming in will please not to meddle with the apparatus or they will get their fingers dirty. Larry will take him out with his shovel and pan when the audience get sick. Song, "Johnny fill up the bowl" by Tute Anderson (a buck Norwegian.)

ALLEN—Prex's pet Sheep. Prof. of skimmed milk and lettuce. This sickly belching booby acts like he was in the habit of cramming too much (his belly.) He gave up teaching Greek because his little mind could not comprehend so *many* (?) things. He never had a definite idea. When asked the simplest question he answers them: I have not—ah! had the—umph! ah! opportunity to—aciough!—look up that—ah! point; my book—ah! has not yet—umph! arrived from—ugh! ah! London.

S(ORT O) H(EADSTRONG) CARPENTER will arise if any audience be left when the spasms have subsided and explain that the exertions just wriggled out are his productions; but they do him no credit; so just to show what an erudite man can do, when he is fed for it, he will fold his hands, close one eye and deliver the prayer on which he worked till half past three o'clock one night; omitting to state that big feet, in an extempore, knocked him out of time next morning.

"A rattling man in his talk is Carp.
An extravagant lover (?) of Prex,
He loves to tell stories, play the jewsharp
And blackguard the opposite sex.

A(SKMENOQUESTION) KERR. This great lubberly wide mouthed specimen of humanity is a cross between an Esquimau and a Hubbard squash. He has no piece to say but will get up, open his mouth from ear to ear and look at the girls. His instruments are a pair of tongs a fine toothed comb a syringe and a microscope with which he examines the patients of the great natural healer John Twombly.

J(UG O) B(EER) FENLING. This philological skunk was imported form Holland at a slight expense. He calls himself a Prof. but is only a Tutor. He is a boorish lubber and being *intimately* acquainted with most of the gals around town, his wife has nary click nor chile. He has become so perfect that he can spit into the neck of a quart mucilage bottle at fifteen yards. This Teutonic ass is also a base sycophant and at Prex's word will kiss the GREAT toe of Wm. Lance Dow Twombly, and flatter him on the *delicacy* of his *feet-ures* and the hugeness of his *understanding*. The town and Milwaukee breweries have been chartered to keep him refreshed on this occasion. Gute! Mein Gott Meester Twombly! Gute! Gute!

OLD NICK. His Satanic magesty will marshal the infernal hosts. He will also engineer in these scenes. He *suckles* frequently. Every vacation he posts off to Washington to see his mistress. When first brought here, the child was in short clothes but has grown up among us to tall coats and running with the girls.

BULLY PARK. This old buck and his mate are as prolific as rabbits. The high toned Prof. tried to run the "Democrat" for a while but the "Journal" made so much fun of him, he got mad and came back to suck his Anna Water. He has got two songs to sing. One he sung to the Freshmen and the other he warbled at the feet of Prex. He will also say Jim Bash is about as smart as I am. Let him only marry into our family and we fellows will populate the world.

J(UMP UP) E(LECTRICAL) DAVIES. This grandiloquent cussate is a complex compound and recent researches have proved him to have been made by Lucifer in a thick black skin by the following reaction. (Brimstone Gas) 14 + a double acetate of (polluted shimmy tails and blue neckties precipitated in grease) 18 (good grinding *gut*) 74½ feet + (decomposed infected mishite) 12 + (acid of devilish conceit) 10 + (hoggish laziness) 9 + (adipose) 7 + (high cockolorum creptals) 6 + (great grunts) 10 — Davies. When he comes, ushers need not furnish him with a seat for he is supported by boils. He has ever been a childless husband but seven long years have not removed the expectation of a guest, to welcome which heir he is now building "*my mansion*."

B(ILLYHELL) DANIELLS. This half weaned skunk calf was driven from the stock-yard at Haward, started west, was lassoed by *Van Slyke* and placed upon the University farm as chief of the diggers. Here he has gained a reputation for extreme littleness, sneakativeness, boorishness and mulishness. If questioned by the audience as to his individuality he will give an evasive answer and relate his hurricane adventure, thus proving the streakedness of winds and if allowed to proceed will tell what he knows about saddle grafting as explained to him about two summers ago by Bishop Whipple at Faribault, Minn. Perhaps he will forget to add that the graft is yet fruitless. As he takes his seat he will propose the following toast. "To the Agricultural College Land Grant and $500 addition to my salary." To be responded to by Irvy.

R(OOTING) D(EVIL) IRVING. This long snouted, crosseyed, long eared, stuff legged hog has been lately kept at the University pen. On account of his strong propensities and the Samsonian power of his snout it has been very difficult to keep him inclosed. He has been during the last year on the whole a regular bore. He once said, "Do not marry young and when you do make a good choice.——" He will on this occasion speak indorsing Danie's views, but will neglect to mention being caught on the doorstep at 11.59 P. M. by the chemical thief.

R(UMBLE GUT) B(ELLY ACHE) ANDERSON. If on this occasion a trembling noise be heard, fear not, for "'tis not the thunder nor the cannon's deafening roar," but the war cry of belly ache in Andersons Norwegian 40 rod contracted gut. He is a footer at the butt end of the Profs. He will come into the hall with his head 4 ft. in advance of his brains. This spider bandy legged, broken backed, cramp bellied, muscled Norwegian buck, will be dangerous to those who will stand in his way to the door when the band plays the tune "Gallop to 10." When Odin calls him to give account of his rip and tear in Norway he will sing "My Father calls me I must go."

R(APSCALLION) H(ELL DESTINED) BROWN. This contemptible niggard, came to the University about ten years ago. His daily food is pickles, chowchow and brick dust. Gastric juice could not work this, which accounts for his slim sorry looking skeleton, a turtive and evil eye and long shape nce with a slightly lifted lip and exposed teeth. He has a slinking appearance a Lover. He got his sheepskin last year by carrying notes to the class written on his shirt sleeves. He delights in Black Crook, White Faun and Lydia Thompson. "Boys what a gay leg." "What lively palpitations," "I wish I was with Annie."

E(MPTY) H(EADED) CRAIG. This young white headed softy is always sneaking around among the Profs. He is of the lowest order of Toots. He offers up his prayers to Toot Anderson every morning. He is not worthy of further notice.

BELLACHE PRAYER by Prof. Kerr.

ROLL UP YOUR BREECHES HERE THEY COME !!

WINDY H. BARLY. Ladies and Gentlemen please notice his pair bolic curors, he is a mathematical calf, sired by Prof. Park. We were not expecting to have him exhibited to day, for we have had him out twice before and he pizzled out behind; but Prof. Park said he must show those curors once more. He is very much confused on the stage if he hears paper rattle he thinks he is at No. 10. Pat will relate to you how he pulled off his tail at the armory two years ago; Davies will show it to you in a bottle at the Cattle "exit." Prex to Carp. in an undertone, who *pooped?*

Be not afraid—It is I, J. WHITFORD BASHFORD, the young demosthenes of the city of Fayette. "I am too sharp for Prex and fooled him nicely on that Freshmen article. [Neglects to state how he sneaked out and threw the responsibility on W.] I can preach three sermons [copied ones] every Sunday and then beat Noyes. I'm a buster, I am. I'll take the first honor." This egotistical blowhard who came here next after Prof. John has at length graduated. By carrying cobs and acting "old Roe" for the faculty, and being a brother Methodist with Prex he has succeeded in taking an honor.

DISTURBANCE.

Deafening roar from the University barn yard; two old oxen are being physicked out of their hids; 'tis too bad but Prex must have boots, nothing else will fit.

FEATHER LEGGED BOYCE. This smooth faced, hypocritical, ungainly, loose jointed, odesifirous, giraffeticus, who is a

Slim and slender, also rotten topped,
Young and tender, loosely gotten up—

boy, in whom total depravity and total want of capillary appendages are plainly depicted upon every feature, is exceedingly loose in morals and manness as well as joints. Thou illmannered and unsophisticated Boy[ce] listen to the council of Odin, when thou hast called for a Lady at the reception room of a Saturday, and a throng of beholders are present

Do not sit in silence panting
But arise and let her know
That you called for her who blushing,
Stands before you all aglow.

FIRE WATER COON. This illigitimate sneaking scoundrel will tell how he came it on his cousin in '69, how he entered Albion school under an assumed name and was kicked out for *doing it*. You brute, debauched drunkard and despised thief, you are answerable for your Edgerton scrape, your drunken night at Stoughton. Pay Maria who lives near Dr. Br——; don't cheat the proprietor of the Elderado as you did men of similar occupation at Stoughton, Edgerton and Janesville.

Following the Civil War, military drill became a familiar part of university life. The Morrill Act required that the university offer military training for male students. Participation grew in the 1870s, when Congress approved funds to establish a full-time professor of military science and tactics. Drill became a requirement for graduation in the 1890s.

One of the university's early catastrophes occurred when the original Science Hall burned in 1884. The building, which had been constructed in 1874–1875 at a cost of eighty thousand dollars, had been an important repository for the university's cultural and scientific collections. The fire destroyed irreplaceable collections from the geological and zoological museums, items from various academic departments, important faculty papers, and valuable paintings from the art gallery. The most notable paintings included a view of Lake Monona and one of Lake Mendota by Thomas Moran, a distinguished painter of the American West.

University instruction in law began in 1868. Students were taught through lectures and participated in a weekly moot court. This composite picture, printed in 1880, shows two individuals who were important figures in the development of the university. Faculty member Colonel William Freeman Vilas served with distinction in the Civil War, as a member of the Wisconsin legislature, and as a United States senator. He was postmaster general and secretary of the interior in the administration of President Grover Cleveland. When he died in 1908, he left a trust to the university which endowed the Vilas research professorships and Vilas scholarships. He is memorialized on campus through Vilas Communication Hall. Robert G. Siebecker was a Madison attorney and the brother-in-law of Robert M. La Follette. He became a judge and later an associate justice of the Wisconsin Supreme Court as well as a curator of the State Historical Society and vice president of the Wisconsin Alumni Association. He is remembered through Siebecker House, a unit of Adams Hall in the Lakeshore Halls complex.

Law Class and Faculty, 1880

Engineering students, shown here in 1881 with their theodolites and marking stakes, have been a familiar sight on the campus for more than a century.

Chi Psi fraternity established the first fraternity house at the university in 1881, at the northwest corner of Frances and Langdon streets. As the popularity of fraternities and sororities grew, they replaced the literary societies as the principal organizational outlet for student interests and activities.

This photo of Delta Gamma sorority, taken in 1887, reveals the style of dress and seriousness of attitude projected by women students of the period.

As enrollment increased, students had to seek lodging in the community rather than on the campus. This picture, taken in 1888, is inscribed on the back: "Partial interior view of room, 123 W. Gilman St. with occupants in a 'brown study.' " The students were Theodore A. Boerner (B.L., 1889) and Horace J. Smith (B.S., 1887; LL.B., 1889). Boerner went on to become a Milwaukee businessman, and Smith, a De Pere attorney.

PRESENTED TO
UNIVERSITY OF WISCONSIN
BY
GEORGE E. WALDO
B.M.E. 1885 - LL.B. 1888

UNIVERSITY OF WISCONSIN BASEBALL TEAM 1886-1887
BACK ROW: ROBERT B.McCOY, JOHN C.GAVENEY, AMBROSE B.WINEGAR, JOHN M.BUNN, DAVID E.SPENCER
FRONT ROW: JAMES McCULLY, CHARLES M.WILLIAMS, EDWARD D.SWINEBURNE, GEORGE E.WALDO, GEORGE T.SIMPSON, CORNELIUS A.HARPER

This photo shows the 1886–1887 UW baseball team. As alumnus and historian George I. Haight explained: "During the Bascom time, baseball was the outstanding college sport. From 1881 to 1887 were the days of the famous battery of Connolly and Waldo. . . . Games were played with Beloit, Racine, Northwestern and other nearby teams. The attendance was sometimes larger, but usually ran about two or three hundred. The price of admission was ordinarily 25¢."

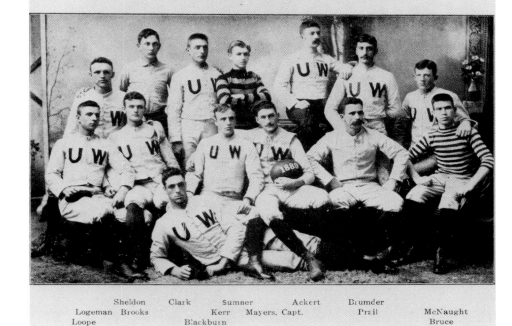

FIRST FOOTBALL SQUAD AT WISCONSIN—SQUAD OF '89

Sheldon	Clark	Sumner	Ackert	Brumder	
Logeman	Brooks	Kerr	Mayers, Capt.	Prail	McNaught
Loope		Blackburn			Bruce

Football appeared in 1889 as part of a broadening of the intercollegiate athletic program. College sports were on the rise and soon became enormously popular among students and townspeople.

History professor William F. Allen (right), one of the early distinguished members of the UW faculty, is shown here with his son, Will, in the study of their home at 228 Langdon Street. Allen joined the faculty in 1867 and served until his death in 1889. He taught ancient and medieval history and was the mentor of Frederick Jackson Turner.

This 1870s view down State Street, looking from the capitol toward University Hall, points to an expanding community and the gradual closing of the distance between the campus and the community.

A
University
Comes
of Age

A sense of change filled the air as John Bascom left the university in 1887. What had been a struggling college had moved toward becoming a university. No one could foresee that the reputation and influence of the university would extend far beyond the confines of the state by the end of the century. Yet tangible signs heralded progress toward a wider recognition of the university's academic development. Bascom's insistence on moral and intellectual integrity had laid the foundation for growth. His accomplishments were reinforced and enhanced by the two men who followed him: Thomas Chrowder Chamberlin and Charles Kendall Adams.

The regents had approached Chamberlin about the university presidency in 1885, at the height of the tension between Bascom and the board. He declined the offer at that time, choosing to continue his work as head of the glacial division of the United States Geological Survey. When he did accept one year later (on the condition that he actually assume the presidency in 1887), he brought a new background to the university. Born in Illinois and educated at Beloit College, he had no immediate ties to the East. His outlook came from the heartland, not New England and the Mid-Atlantic states. He also had developed an impeccable scholarly reputation as he pursued his career as a field geologist.

As president, Chamberlin advanced a number of ideas and concepts that reflected the changing world beyond the campus. He felt that knowledge was not just for scholars but also for the people. Students should be trained in a discipline or for the professions and have the opportunity to broaden their knowledge through elective courses. He also promoted graduate study as a stimulant to research.

Under Chamberlin, the university began to attract scholars of national reputation, such as the economist and social scientist Richard T. Ely. Chamberlin was the first to promote university extension, noting that through this activity "and by publication . . . the University is bringing itself into immediate contact with the people and so educating a very much larger percentage of its natural constituency than before."

Chamberlin's tenure as president was comparatively short. He resigned in 1892 to become head of the geology department at the University of Chicago. Before leaving, however, he pointed the university toward increased maturity and achievement. His successor, Charles Kendall Adams, continued to build a faculty of substantial scholarly achievement. Faculty appointments were carefully scrutinized as a crucial part of the effort to achieve academic distinction.

Adams also moved to fill another important university need. Dramatic growth—enrollment had more than doubled between 1888 and 1895—dictated the need for a major increase in facilities. Adams recognized that establishing effective and cordial relations with the legislature was the key to achieving and sustaining growth. He noted that "the people, through their representatives, must approve and furnish the means of carrying the work forward."

While he could be abrupt on occasion, Adams was generally congenial to the various groups he worked with and had the skill to garner broad support for his programs. He enjoyed various aspects of student life, particularly intercollegiate athletics. He and his wife, who shared his affinity for social activities, successfully developed close relationships with important state and civic leaders, who helped advance the cause of the university. While his relations with the faculty were sometimes strained, Adams received their respect because of his effectiveness in promoting the university on all fronts. He advanced the building program, securing a new library which was incorporated into the new building being constructed to house the State Historical Society. Other important additions included the Law Building, Soils Building, and the Armory.

The Adams initiative carried the university into the new century but ended abruptly in 1900, when Adams's health broke and he asked for a leave of absence. His condition did not improve as he had hoped. Realizing he could not adequately resume his duties, he resigned the presidency in October 1901. Reluctant to accept his resignation, the regents postponed formal action until January 1902. In the meantime, Adams traveled to California to recuperate, but his health had been permanently impaired. He died there in 1902.

In a memorial address, Professor Edward A. Birge, dean of the College of Letters and Science, who had been called to serve as acting president, summarized Adams's contribution: "He heightened the spirit and temper of the teaching given by the University, and elevated the educational ideals which inspired it. Thus his administration not only enlarged the material resources of the University and increased its size, but effected an even more important advance in its inner life."

The university budget proved to be the most tangible measure of growth and change during the Adams era. It tripled during the period, rising from $227,000 in 1887 to $675,000 in 1903. The increased funding represented a broadening of income sources and pointed to an expanding influence of the university in the life of the state. Funds came from the original land endowments; contributions for various programs from the federal government (stimulated by the 1862 Morrill Act); income from student fees, tuition, room rents, and sale of products from the University Experiment Station; gifts and bequests; and state appropriations. This last category represented the most significant expansion of university funding.

In the early years the university's principal operating revenue came from the sale of lands and from tuition and fees. That pattern changed with the 1876 legislation which gave the university a proportionate share of the state's property tax income. As the wealth of the state began to increase, the legislature became alarmed at the potential for growth in this area. The university's share of tax income could increase significantly as the economy expanded. This increase would be unaccompanied by any external oversight of expenditures. A new means for accountability had to be found. The legislature voted in 1899 to appropriate a specific amount each year to finance university expenditures. This move increased legislative control as it reduced the influence of the regents. At the same time, it provided a means for determining which aspects of the university's operation were being funded by direct state appropriation.

Increased enrollment and funding generated an expansion of the faculty and the range of subjects taught. The achievements of some faculty members gained wide recognition, like those of Stephen M. Babcock and Frederick Jackson Turner. Babcock came to the university from the New York Agricultural Experiment Station in 1887. In 1890 he perfected an apparatus to test the butterfat content of milk. The Babcock Test offered a simple, accurate, and consistent method for determining the quality and commercial value of any milk sample. A Wisconsin native, Turner had studied history as an undergraduate at the university under William F. Allen, earned his doctorate at Johns Hopkins University, and returned to join the UW faculty. At the 1893 meeting of the American Historical Association held in Chicago, he read his paper "The Significance of the Frontier in American History," which had a central influence on the study of American history for decades.

As excellent scholars came to the university, day-to-day administrative matters became more complex, and knowledge grew in specialized fields. The curriculum, which had been continually evolving since the close of the Civil War, increasingly emphasized the practical and vocational aspects of learning. The broadening curriculum and the increase in the number of disciplines led in 1889 to the establishment of four colleges: Letters and Science, Mechanics and Engineering, Law, and Pharmacy. The development continued with the establishment of the School of Economics, Political Science, and History in 1892 and the School of Music during the 1894–1895 academic year. In 1899 the regents approved inauguration of the summer session, which began informally more than a decade earlier as a joint venture between the university and the Wisconsin Teachers Association. These developments led to an increased administrative profile, as deans and directors were appointed to oversee the development of curricula and programs.

At the same time, the faculty governance pioneered under Bascom became a distinctive feature of university life. So did the principle of academic freedom, as a landmark episode established the right of faculty members to pursue the truth free of political interference. The person called to Wisconsin to organize the new School of Economics, Political Science, and History was Richard T. Ely, a distinguished professor of economics at Johns Hopkins University. A letter published in the July 12, 1894, issue of the *Nation* magazine by Oliver E. Wells, state superintendent of public instruction, accused Ely of fomenting strikes and boycotts and advocating "utopian, impractical, or pernicious doctrines." The regents appointed a special committee to investigate the matter, since Wells was a member of the board.

The regent committee delivered its report on September 18, 1894. It declared Wells's charges without foundation. At the encouragement of Regent John M. Olin, the report contained an additional section which dealt with the general question of academic freedom. The report pointed out that the university faculty during the previous eighteen months had written nearly two hundred books, pamphlets, and magazine articles which represented a wide variety of thought and opinion. The regents concluded:

> In all lines of academic investigation it is of the utmost importance that the investigator should be absolutely free to follow the indications of truth wherever they may lead.

> Whatever may be the limitations which trammel inquiry elsewhere, we believe that the great state University of Wisconsin should ever encourage that continual and fearless sifting and winnowing by which alone the truth can be found.

As further testament of their conviction, the regents adopted a resolution censuring Wells.

A change in the makeup of the student population accompanied the change in the faculty profile. Enrollment increased rapidly during this period, rising from 612 in the fall of 1887 to nearly 2,000 by the turn of the century. Although they still came primarily from the middle class, the students represented a broader geographic distribution. And with increased emphasis on scholarship and research, graduate students composed a growing percentage.

The outward aspects of student life were changing, too. Student publications displaced some of the influence of the literary societies. The student yearbook the *Trochos* (a Greek approximation for the word *badger*) appeared in 1885. It became the *Badger* in 1889 and subsequently served as an important annual measure of the scope and substance of student life. After several earlier newspapers, such as the *Aegis* and the *University Press*, had come and gone, the *Daily Cardinal*, founded in 1892, rapidly became a prominent forum for student thought and opinion as well as a means for providing a sense of identity for the expanding student population.

Intercollegiate athletics also came to prominence during this period. Success in track and crew gained recognition for the university. The Wisconsin football team was particularly successful during the last decade of the century, spurred on by the sensational achievements of Pat O'Dea, the fabled "Kangaroo Kicker" from Australia.

Enthusiasm for intercollegiate athletics demonstrated that schools would go to extensive lengths to compete with their rivals. With no eligibility rules for participants, athletes enrolled to participate in sports rather than to worry about making satisfactory progress toward a degree. Some freely transferred from one college to the next, plying their talents wherever they would be in the greatest demand. Townspeople saw the intercollegiate rivalries as an entertaining way of pitting one university community against another. Gambling and drunkenness at the games were a common occurrence.

The faculty were initially indifferent, but this attitude changed quickly as it became evident that the popularity of intercollegiate athletics took students' minds away from the classroom. A special committee on athletics, created in 1889, adopted specific eligibility rules in 1894. The faculty concern about athletics was a regional phenomenon. In January 1895 President Smart of Purdue University called for a meeting in Chicago to consider what could be done to regulate intercollegiate athletics. This meeting led to the formation in February 1896 of a controlling organization, consisting of faculty representatives from Chicago, Illinois, Michigan, Minnesota, Northwestern, Purdue, and Wisconsin. The new organization, called the Intercollegiate Conference of Faculty Representatives, adopted uniform procedures for athletic competition among the cooperating universities. While the Intercollegiate Conference remains the official name of the organization, it became more commonly known as the Big Ten when additional schools joined the conference.

Increased enrollment also had an important effect on student activity during this period. Available dormitory space diminished dramatically. Students lived in private rooming houses or in the accommodations offered by the Greek-letter societies. Students also formed study and improvement associations, founded a book-buying cooperative, and tried to establish a student health service.

As the number of students increased, so did their visibility—both on the campus and in the community. In previous years the president invariably served as the final arbiter of student discipline. The rise in the numbers of students made that task more difficult and impractical. The faculty stepped forward to assume a greater responsibility for controlling student social activities. They made the rules and recommended appropriate penalties to the regents. For the most part, they dealt with the type of student transgressions which have characterized the species since Socrates held forth in the Groves of Academe: drunkenness, gambling, carousing, cheating on examinations, and general rowdiness. The rowdiness occasionally took on menacing overtones, however. Hazing became increasingly troublesome, and continuing and sometimes severe tension existed between police and students. Students periodically would march up State Street disrupting traffic. In January 1899 they marched into the Fuller Opera House and stopped the show. In October some male students and "city hoodlums" made an incursion into Ladies Hall and took articles of clothing from the laundry and student rooms.

The era 1888–1903 saw the introduction of extension services as an important means of taking the university to the people of the state, although it was not to experience a full flowering until the Van Hise administration. The Chautauqua program of adult education initiated in New York in 1874 featured lectures, institutes, and summer programs. It stimulated development of a similar activity at the university in 1885 with the establishment of the short course and related farmers' institutes. The success of these programs led rapidly to other developments, including the initiation of a summer session for teachers, the establishment of mechanics' institutes, and the offering of university lectures, which Chamberlin estimated involved as many as 8,500 people and embraced fifty different subjects.

Adams continued the commitment to extension activity by overseeing the initiation of correspondence courses and appointing a full-time secretary to look after the various programs. The initial impetus, however, wavered: according to historian Reuben Gold Thwaites, "Many of the most eminent professors in the University are reluctant to engage in this work, which involves the hardships of long railway journeys and interferes with their studies." This attitude sent the extension program into a short-lived period of dormancy at the close of the century. New initiatives, however, would soon emerge in this and other areas which further expanded the university's growing national reputation.

This portion of an 1885 bird's-eye view of Madison done by Norris, Wellge and Company, Milwaukee, for a local implement dealer, S. L. Sheldon, shows Bascom Hill as the principal campus area with the eastern boundary of the campus marked by Park Street. The drawing reveals that the Lower Campus was still a relatively undefined part of the university landscape.

By 1895 the configuration of University Hall had changed considerably. The dome had been embellished, and the Italianate rounded portico had been removed and replaced with a square, more classical version. Most important, a south wing had been added to provide additional classroom and administrative space.

This photograph, taken between 1895 and 1900, reveals the growth of both Madison and the university. Familiar buildings include Holy Redeemer church and school in the right foreground and the Red Gym and Science Hall beyond. University Hall with its dome and remodeled portico occupies its familiar stately position on College Hill. University Heights in the background at left is still largely undeveloped.

State Street became a well-established thoroughfare by the turn of the century. This photo, taken at State and Park streets in 1896, shows the various modes of transportation available at the time.

The University Boathouse, constructed in 1892, and the Gymnasium and Armory, completed in 1894, served as focal points for recreational and athletic activity. The Wisconsin Crew, which used an adjunct to the boathouse as its headquarters, competed with considerable success against eastern schools as the university's intercollegiate athletics program expanded in the last decade of the century.

This view, looking south along the Park Street boardwalk, was taken near Science Hall at the turn of the century.

The Law Building, designed by Charles S. Frost and completed in 1893, featured a modified Richardsonian Romanesque style. A 1940 addition accommodated the expanding law library. In the 1960s a modern, more spacious facility replaced the original building.

This residence, located at 10 North Babcock Drive, was built in 1897 to serve as the home of the dean of the College of Agriculture. The row of trees bisecting the photo a short distance beyond the house outlines the path of Elm Drive, an important campus geographic axis for nearly a century.

This photo, taken in the early 1890s, shows the gradual westward extension of the campus. The house in the right foreground served as the first official president's residence from 1866 to 1878. Washburn Observatory was built in 1878 and given to the university by former governor Cadwallader C. Washburn. Hiram Smith Hall, at left below the slope of the hill, was completed in 1892 and served as the headquarters for the dairy school. It is purported to be "the first dairy building constructed in the western hemisphere."

This house at 772 Langdon Street served as the president's residence from 1887 until 1925, when it was razed to make way for construction of the Memorial Union.

The Dairy Barn, built in 1897, features a picturesque architectural style commonly seen in the Normandy region of France. It and King Hall were the sites of pioneering research on vitamins and on nonprotein nitrogen used by ruminant animals, and engineering research on silos, silage, and barn ventilation. The ramp at right provided a convenient way of getting hay into the barn.

This view shows the western slope of Observatory Hill. Hiram Smith Hall is at right. The College of Agriculture heating plant is in the center. Behind is the Soils Building, completed in 1894 and later named King Hall after Franklin Hiram King, first professor of agricultural and soil physics in the United States, who served twenty-two years as a faculty member until his death in 1911.

This view of College Hill shows how the main campus had matured in approximately fifty years.

In this view southwest from the top of the hill, signs of further progress are apparent. The construction of the Wisconsin General Hospital displaced the homes in the foreground in the 1920s. The property beyond was purchased by the university in 1893 for development as an athletic field. The grandstand and track surrounding the playing field (left center) are prominent features in that area. The emerging development of University Heights is obvious in the background. The new subdivision was a 106-acre tract purchased in 1893 by a group of wealthy Madison men led by W. T. Fish.

Although development of the city of Madison proceeded rapidly in the latter part of the nineteenth century, reminders of the frontier still existed in the area. This 1895 photograph shows an occupied Winnebago Indian wigwam located just south of Lake Wingra in the area that is now part of the University Arboretum.

Sophomores Carlos Rider of Racine and William Broughton of Dwight, Illinois, are pictured in a Langdon Street rooming house. Evidently, undergraduate life in the mid-1890s occasionally featured a background of banjo and guitar music.

Military drill had been a part of university life since 1866. This photograph, taken in 1893, shows a lingering influence of the Civil War in the officers' dress and equipment.

Coeducation in all aspects of university life became an accomplished fact by the mid-1890s. This photo depicts a relaxed and somewhat informal group of university women students.

Literary societies, featuring the joint debate, were initially the most important student activity. They gradually began to lose their attraction as intercollegiate athletics and Greek-letter societies gained prominence in the 1890s. Theodore Kronshage, shown at upper right of this 1893 photo, received bachelor's and law degrees from the university. He practiced law in Milwaukee and later became chairman of the Wisconsin Public Service Commission. He served as a member and president of the board of regents in the 1920s and was active in the establishment of the residence halls system. The Kronshage units in the Lakeshore Halls area honor his memory.

The last two decades of the century saw the rise of student musical groups, including the Glee Club and the Banjo and Mandolin Club (pictured here). The groups made periodic out-of-town trips to entertain. Mostly they traveled to nearby locations, but occasionally they ranged as far west as Denver or as far east as Ann Arbor, Michigan.

Students had time for fun and frivolity as the century was coming to a close and the university was maturing. Selections from Badger yearbooks of the period also reveal the changing aspects of student fashion.

CHOLLIE—Aw, Fweddie, deah boy, caw'n't youw let me take youw knife?
FREDDIE—Certainly, old fellow, but you're not going to commit suicide?
CHOLLIE—Aw, no, my deah boy, I want to cut that beastly Psych. exam., doncher know.

Development of a women's athletic program followed soon after the establishment of men's intercollegiate athletics. This picture of the 1899 women's basketball team shows uniforms that were decorous, but hardly suitable for a fast-moving floor game. The team competed against local high schools and a college in Milwaukee.

During the latter part of the century the university's general library was located at the rear of Music Hall. The collection included over 51,000 bound volumes and 15,000 unbound pamphlets. Students had to pay a two-dollar deposit before they could borrow books. Other collections were housed in the law library and the Woodman Astronomical Library in Washburn Observatory. Students also had access to the collections of the State Historical Society, which contained over 104,000 volumes and 100,000 pamphlets.

One of the university's preeminent faculty members of the late 1800s was Frederick Jackson Turner. A Wisconsin native and university alumnus, Turner became a widely respected historian and actively partici-pated in a number of faculty governance issues. He is shown here meeting his American history seminar at the Historical Library in the state capitol during the 1893–1894 academic year.

As the university matured, its instructional program became more complex and diverse. This photo of a zoological lecture room in Science Hall shows a number of teaching aids. As a university catalog of the time explains, "For illustrating the lectures in botany and in zoology, there are Auzoux models, both of plants and animals, an electric projecting lantern and microscope, over 600 lantern slides, a large number of wall charts, microscope slides, etc."

This photo shows a biology laboratory in Science Hall at the turn of the century. The woman standing at left is Leila Bascom (a distant cousin of John Bascom), who later became an associate professor of English in the Extension Division and an active participant in Madison civic affairs.

Faculty may come and go, but janitors endure. At least that appeared to be the case with Patrick K. Walsh, a native of Ireland who came to Madison in 1857 as a roofer and subsequently was employed from 1861 to his death in 1897 as a janitor for the university and a messenger for the president. The Daily Cardinal offered this eulogy following his death: "The life of Patrick Walsh shows to us, after all, it is character rather than scholarship that has influence. . . . He made himself a part of the institution, a repository of its traditions, to be known, remembered, and loved by the graduates."

These young men are not members of some mystic religious order, but dairy students pictured around 1900. The dairy program began in 1889 and featured instruction in the operation of a creamery under the guidance of Professor Stephen M. Babcock. Students manufactured and sold products on the campus and to local markets—a tradition which continues today.

Football great Pat O'Dea is a legendary figure in Wisconsin athletics. The "Kangaroo Kicker" came to Madison from Australia in the late 1890s at the urging of his brother, Andrew, the UW crew coach. Pat's most enduring record is a sixty-three-yard drop kick against Northwestern in 1899. O'Dea disappeared during World War I and was presumed lost. In 1934 he was discovered living quietly under an assumed name in northern California. The discovery provided an opportunity for the Alumni Association to bring him back to the campus for Homecoming of that same year, when his athletic exploits were again celebrated.

This 1894 composite portrait of "lady instructors" shows that women were being integrated into the instructional program during the period when coeducation was becoming an established part of university life.

This 1884 photo of the mechanics and engineering faculty may seem little more than a sampler of popular facial hairstyles of the time. It does, however, contain portraits of three individuals who would soon become key university administrators: Charles R. Van Hise, the university's eighth president, is pictured at far left, center row; Charles Sumner Slichter, dean of the Graduate School from 1920 to 1934, second from left, bottom row; and Frederick E. Turneaure, dean of the College of Engineering from 1903 to 1937, second from left, top row.

The university's sixth president, Thomas C. Chamberlin (1887–1892), took steps to solidify the university's academic position, as graduate programs and new disciplines were introduced during his administration. A distinguished scientist, Chamberlin left Wisconsin to become head of the department of geology at the University of Chicago.

Charles Kendall Adams succeeded Chamberlin as president, serving from 1892 to 1901. President and Mrs. Adams were known for their gracious hospitality. This photo of Adams in his study in the President's House at the corner of Park and Langdon streets reflects the inviting warmth the Adamses projected.

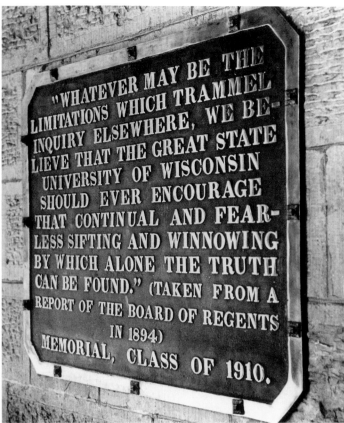

The university's famous "sifting and winnowing" statement, memorialized on the plaque given by the class of 1910, is a quote from a report approved by the regents following an investigation of the controversial teachings advanced by economics professor Richard T. Ely, pictured above.

President Adams is believed to have drafted the statement characterized as "the University's Magna Carta" of academic freedom. The plaque did not gain immediate acceptance when first offered, since some members of the board of regents considered its proclamation too radical and provocative. The regents did not officially accept the gift for two years,

temporarily relegating the plaque to the basement of University Hall. Following considerable discussion and political maneuverings, the plaque was resurrected after the regents approved a resolution allowing it to be mounted on the building in 1915 in conjunction with the fifth reunion of the class of 1910.

Professor Stephen M. Babcock made an early and important university contribution to science when he developed the first reliable butterfat tester in 1890. He is shown here (right) demonstrating his testing device to agriculture dean William A. Henry and President Thomas C. Chamberlin. In 1989 a poll conducted by the Milwaukee Sentinel *listed Babcock eighth in a selection of the ten "most significant and influential personalities in the state's history."*

In 1894 bacteriologist Harry L. Russell conducted a dramatic demonstration before hundreds of dairymen and breeders gathered at the Stock Pavilion. Russell ordered a substantial number of the university's dairy herd slaughtered and then performed autopsies to show that the cows, who appeared to have been perfectly healthy, were actually infected with tuberculosis. Russell's research and educational efforts led to the passage of legislation and the development of tests to eliminate the disease from Wisconsin dairy herds.

The
Wisconsin
Idea
in Action

As the regents sought a successor to Charles Kendall Adams in 1903, they looked both outside and inside the university. Several outside candidates turned down the position. The prime internal candidate was acting president Edward A. Birge, but he did not campaign for the job. Governor Robert M. La Follette made no effort to disguise his support of Charles R. Van Hise. The regents were reluctant to introduce politics into the search. When they did vote, however, they chose Van Hise, with Birge coming in a close second.

Both La Follette and Van Hise were members of the class of 1879. La Follette had gained prominence as a student debater and orator. After he graduated from the university he went on to practice law and pursue a career in politics. Van Hise chose the scholarly life. The first person to receive the Ph.D. degree from the university (in 1892), he gained distinction in his field of geology—as director of the Lake Superior Division of the United States Geological Survey and as a member of the university faculty.

La Follette and Van Hise shared not only their undergraduate experience but also the feeling that the university should lend its resources to the development of the state and its people, particularly in promoting legislative and administrative reform in government. This attitude formed the basis of the concept that was soon to be identified as the Wisconsin Idea.

Van Hise was inaugurated on June 5, 1904, as part of the university's Jubilee marking the fiftieth anniversary of the first commencement. Shortly after his inauguration, Van Hise set the tenor of his administration when he said, "I shall never be content until the beneficent influence of the University reaches every home in the state." A later variation included the clause "and the boundaries of our campus are coextensive with the boundaries of our State." This educational philosophy had been prominently connected with the development of the university extension program during the administration of President Chamberlin. In 1907 Van Hise gave the program a distinct identity by naming Louis E. Reber dean of the extension department after securing a direct appropriation of twenty thousand dollars from the legislature. Reber emphasized the university's traditional academic strengths as a means of dealing with utilitarian concerns. The idea obviously struck a responsive chord in the legislature: the appropriation for the extension program rose consistently throughout the Van Hise era.

Dean Reber put together a staff that carried the program throughout the state. While faculty had become increasingly reluctant to make regular educational trips into the state because of the impact on their own research and teaching, other means emerged for transmitting knowledge to the people. Professor William H. Lighty organized correspondence courses. Agricultural Extension agents acted as circuit riders, carrying information to the far reaches of the state. Additional penetration came later through the development of wireless telegraphy and radio broadcasting.

Not all university developments moved so smoothly from a political standpoint as the extension program. Throughout the Van Hise years, there was a continuing battle for control of the Republican party between the reform-minded progressives and the conservative stalwarts. This continuing struggle had an obvious influence on the university and provided an ongoing challenge to Van Hise. He attempted to achieve growth and expansion without creating a political firestorm that might cripple his program. He sought ways to establish institutional and educational principles, but at the same time he recognized the need for political expediency.

The need for state support was continuous, and Van Hise pointed out that "if the university of Wisconsin is to do for the state what it has a right to expect, it must develop, expand, strengthen creative work at whatever cost." Not everyone was enthusiastic. Governor James O. Davidson (1906–1911), who replaced La Follette when the latter was elected to the United States Senate, appeared to dislike Van Hise. Nevertheless, Davidson showed no inclination to intercede and modify Van Hise's program.

A direct challenge came from the board of regents, comprised predominantly of Republican stalwarts. By 1909 the regents had inserted themselves into personnel and curriculum matters. They also closely scrutinized teaching and downplayed research in all fields but the applied sciences. These incursions led to at least one crucial defection: Frederick Jackson Turner left for Harvard in the fall of 1909 in reaction to the regents' forays. After investigation and discussion of the charges that they were unduly involved in the academic affairs of the faculty, the regents pulled back. Following a meeting of a regent-faculty conference committee, the regents avowed that they had "no intention of interfering with the customary methods of educational administration by the faculty." They also stated that the faculty would assume "the initiative in formulating educational policies" and that appointments were "to be made through the regular channels as developed in the custom of the University."

Van Hise worked to focus the regents' energy on the business aspects of the university and kept them occupied with facts and figures which he used to outline and explain the university's needs. While this ploy and faculty resistance subdued the regents' involvement in academic concerns, it did not protect the university from others. A major political struggle arose over the question of "efficiency" in education, the control of education in the public schools, and the training of teachers. In 1913 the legislature directed the state's board of public affairs to study the university's "efficiency of teaching and educational methods." William Harvey Allen, a director of the New York Bureau of Municipal Research, was chosen to conduct a survey for this purpose.

The Allen Survey rapidly proved to be a political football. The survey's major premise was "that the most important single need of the university is scientific attention to management." The assumption was based on a wide-ranging and often unfocused number of findings. After the regents received a copy of the survey in November 1914, Dean Birge and Professor George Clarke Sellery asked that the report and its exhibits not be accepted without an independent outside review and comments from the university. They questioned Allen's research capabilities and methods and characterized the evaluation as "an inextricable tangle of 'facts' and 'conclusions.'" They further cautioned that "no statement of facts and no conclusion of Dr. Allen can be accepted without verification."

Striving for objectivity, the board of public affairs decided to conduct its own inquiry. Meanwhile, various commentators questioned the whole idea of "efficiency" in higher education: their skeptical reactions appeared in such publications as the *New York Evening Post*, the *Nation*, the *Dial*, and *Current Opinion*.

The survey died a slow political death as Allen lobbied for influence with Governor Emanuel Philipp (1915–1921) but failed to gain any political leverage with the legislature. Eventually Allen left the state to pursue other interests. The principal residual effect of the survey for the university was to stimulate the formation of study committees to review and suggest possible improvements. The areas of investigation included research, graduate study and fieldwork, instruction, foreign language requirements, physical plant, faculty records, and faculty organization.

Governor Philipp, in the meantime, seized the opportunity to push for the creation of a single board to oversee public education in the state. Van Hise opposed the move, as did others. The bill designed to establish a single board was gradually weakened by amendments. In its final form, it created a five-member state board of education but left the regents with the power to govern the university.

The practices used to grant outside speakers access to the campus offer a further indication of the political tenor of the university. Van Hise periodically found himself in choppy waters when it came to granting a university platform to various controversial speakers of the day. Initially, the president steadfastly maintained that the campus should be open to speakers who advocated unpopular causes or doctrines. When the anarchist Emma Goldman came to Madison at the invitation of the local student Socialist club, cries of alarm sounded. Her appearance was used to support the argument that socialism and anarchism were taught on campus. The board of visitors conducted an inquiry and found no evidence to support the charge.

In 1917, however, Van Hise blocked the campus appearance of the Socialist Max Eastman before the Wisconsin Forum, a student organization dedicated to the discussion of controversial issues not normally covered in the classroom. Van Hise claimed that his action was not an attack on free speech, but that the university did not allow its facilities to be used as "a platform on which to spread propaganda." That same year, he also criticized Robert M. La Follette, his old friend and classmate, for his refusal to vote for the United States' declaration of war.

While the political storms rose and subsided, the academic program changed and grew. Increased concentration on research became a prime component of university activity. The country needed skilled individuals to operate and manage a society driven by technological change. Technology generated new knowledge and provided for its rapid dissemination. The faculty identified new fields of study and incorporated them into the university curricula. They established departments of sociology, pharmacology, experimental breeding (genetics), and plant pathology, and they introduced courses in social work as well as professionally oriented courses in journalism and library science. Later, in 1926, the university became the first in the nation to offer an undergraduate degree in dance education.

Administrative changes reflected the growing compartmentalization of knowledge. The schools of Pharmacy, Commerce, and Education and the School of Economics and

Political Science were folded into the College of Letters and Science, while home economics moved from the College of Letters and Science to Agriculture. The establishment of a graduate division in 1904 underscored the importance of research and graduate study. When George Comstock was appointed dean of the Graduate School ten years later, graduate enrollment had increased from 115 to 492 students. The Medical School began with a two-year program in 1907 but expanded to offer a four-year course in 1925, as the university began to award the M.D. degree.

The university, which had been historically concerned about its role in training teachers for state schools, moved to establish a program that would treat teaching with a high degree of professionalism. The department of education was reorganized in 1908. Three years later, undergraduate and graduate programs in teacher training emphasized teaching as a lifetime career, not a transitional undertaking on the way to something else. In 1911 the university established the Wisconsin High School as a practice school.

Other signs of change came through the prominence of issues that affected the basic nature and purpose of the university. Many faculty members felt that intercollegiate athletics had grown to such a point that it corrupted the academic purpose of the university. They were so concerned about the problem of overemphasis that they cut back the football schedule from ten to five games during the period 1906–1910. Meanwhile, strict conference rules had been established on residence, eligibility, and university attendance for athletes. In spite of this reformist zeal, student and public enthusiasm for college sports continued to grow. The UW baseball team traveled to Japan in 1909, and the Homecoming ceremony was inaugurated in 1911. The publication of "On, Wisconsin" as the university's official fight song in 1909 also stimulated enthusiasm.

Edward A. Birge noted that during the fifteen years Van Hise was president, the university's income quadrupled: the state appropriation rose from $427,000 in 1903 to $1,600,000 in 1918. Buildings and equipment valued at nearly $300,000 were added during the period. At the same time, a 1908 campus plan for physical development influenced the growth of the campus for the next several decades. The size of the faculty rose from less than 200 to more than 750, and the degrees awarded during the period numbered over 8,700 first degrees and more than 2,100 higher degrees.

In the course of this progress the sudden and unanticipated death of Van Hise in November 1918 came as a profound shock. Van Hise had entered the hospital for routine surgery but developed unforeseen complications and died two days later. His death produced a leadership crisis similar to the one that had occurred when Charles Kendall Adams had become ill in 1900. As they had done previously, the regents looked to Edward A. Birge to provide reliable stewardship in a time of transition. Birge had served as acting president from 1900 to 1903 after Adams had been unable to continue and subsequently resigned. Although Birge had lost the presidency to Van Hise earlier, there was no equivocation this time. He was named president less than a month after Van Hise's death.

It was obvious from the beginning that Birge's presidency would be transitional. Birge took the job at age sixty-seven with the understanding that the regents would search for a much younger man who could be expected to hold the office for an extended period. The regents searched but after a year asked Birge to withdraw his contingency. There was work to be done, and the experience, professional competency, and dedication Birge brought to the job were essential.

The new president concentrated on short-term problems rather than long-range plans. Following World War I, the student population grew considerably, putting a strain on resources. Birge hesitated to make changes that would increase the difficulty for a successor to initiate new programs or to change old ones. He championed student causes but, like Van Hise, encountered difficulty over his handling of controversial speakers invited to campus. As the 1920s unfolded, it became apparent that the time had come to pass the power of the presidency to a younger person. The regents moved in 1924 to establish a committee to seek a replacement for Birge. The most prominent candidate was Dean Roscoe Pound of the Harvard Law School. But Pound saw his future in law and not in the administration of a large public university. The regents then approached a candidate from outside academia: Glenn Frank, age thirty-seven, editor of the *Century Magazine*, came highly recommended by Regent Zona Gale. Frank was appointed president at a special meeting of the regents on May 29, 1925, and assumed his duties on September 1. The regents expected that he would bring to the university the same kind of enthusiasm and accomplishment he had demonstrated as a wunderkind in the publishing world.

Birge left the presidency with an extensive record of dedicated service. He had been a member of the faculty for nearly fifty years. He had twice served as acting president and had been dean of the university's largest college. His accomplishments as president were unsensational but important. Throughout his association with the university, which continued until his death in 1950 at age ninety-nine, Birge pursued a career as a scholar of substantial influence. His research, primarily centered on the biological aspects of Lake Mendota, earned him the title of Father of Limnology in North America. His influence continued through the subsequent work of scholars and ultimately led to the establishment of such important university research centers as the Laboratory for Limnology and the Sea Grant Institute.

The replica of Adolph Weinman's statue of Abraham
Lincoln became a regular
feature of the Bascom Hill
landscape in 1909, when
alumnus and regent Thomas E.
Brittingham, Sr., presented it as
a gift to the university. Originally the statue was placed
approximately one hundred feet
down from the crest of the hill.

It was relocated in 1918, when
it was moved closer to University Hall and surrounded by a
marble exedra. This photo
shows workmen constructing
the semicircular exedra and
steps. During the course of the
construction, the workers
discovered the remains of two
bodies—those of a workman
killed by lightning while

building the first state capitol in
Madison in 1838 and a
companion who had died
earlier. Since College Hill had
served as Madison's first
cemetery, the bones were
reinterred and the graves
marked by grooves in the
cement and two small brass
plates.

UNIVERSITY OF WISCONSIN
GENERAL · DESIGN
FOR FUTURE CONSTRUCTIONAL DEVELOPMENT
WARREN POWERS LAIRD
PAUL PHILIPPE CRET
ARTHUR PEABODY

The most sweeping architectural plan for the university was completed in 1908. As university architect Arthur Peabody explained, "The design attempts to forecast and visualize the physical development of the University during the next forty or fifty years, by laying out in a large ground plan the general form and location of departmental buildings in their logical groups. It is aimed to secure harmony of aspect among groups through emphasizing their unity as parts of one great University. The plan determines the prevailing architectural style." Although certain changes were made in ensuing years, the general pattern of campus development followed the original plan.

THE BIOLOGICAL GROUP

Paul Cret, who collaborated with Peabody and Warren Laird in developing the 1908 plan, drew this sketch to illustrate a design possibility for the grouping of buildings related to the study of biology. The design reflects the beaux-arts style popular at the time.

A dramatic fire of unknown origin destroyed the University Hall dome on the morning of October 10, 1916. Students and university employees assisted in removing equipment from the building and fighting the fire, which was controlled before it could spread to other parts of the building. The total cost of the damage, estimated at twenty-five thousand dollars, was covered by the state insurance fund. The dome was not replaced after the fire, giving the building a less ornate, more subdued appearance.

Students in animal husbandry had to learn a variety of skills and techniques, including the intricacies of braiding a horse's mane. This distinctive training aid, which looks like a precursor of Dr. Doolittle's "Push me, pull you" creature, provided an opportunity for students to develop their skills on a passive subject before tackling a more animated one.

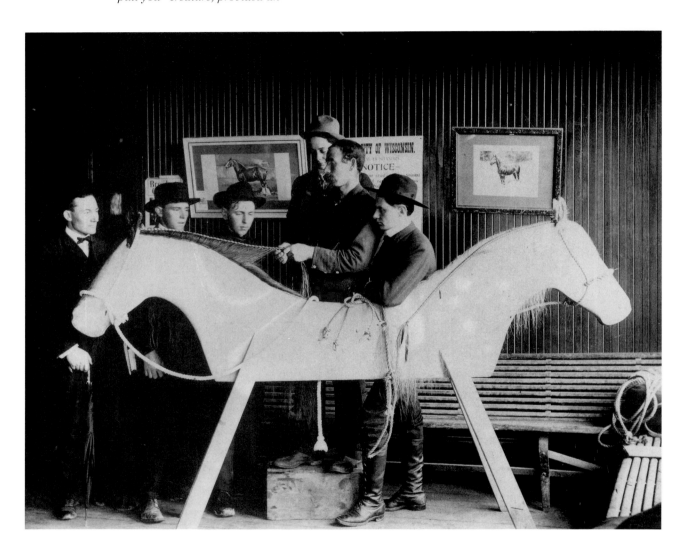

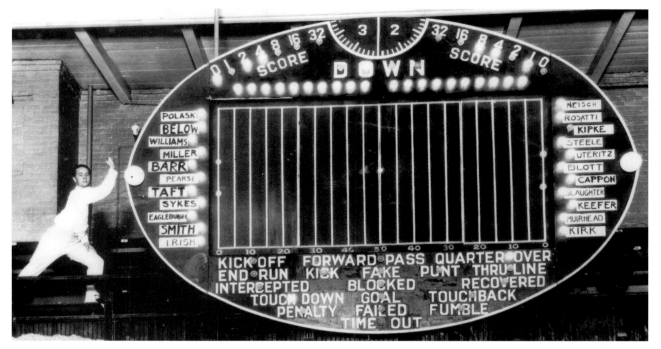

Before radio and television became widely available, football fans were treated to a novel way of following out-of-town games. The "gridograph" was installed in the Red Gym in 1922. A fan paid a twenty-five-cent admission fee to watch as a nimble operator moved a light over the field to mimic the progress of the game described by an account transmitted via telegraph.

Winter Week has been a popular event in the university calendar at various times since 1919, when a ski jump was built on Muir Knoll just west of the university pumping station. A steel structure replaced the original wooden jump in 1932. This was eventually dismantled to make way for the Limnology Laboratory, which presently occupies the former site of the ski jump runway at the bottom of the knoll.

For many, President Charles R. Van Hise was figuratively a man on horseback who provided leadership during a time when the university gained international prominence. On a more practical level, Van Hise, like other men of Madison, used his horse as a convenient mode of getting around the campus and the city. This 1916 photo was probably taken as he viewed a student military maneuver near Eagle Heights and University Bay Marsh.

Edward A. Birge had a long and distinguished career as an administrator, serving as the first dean of the College of Letters and Science, as acting president, and ultimately as president of the university from 1918 to 1925. At the same time, he was a scientist of considerable achievement. His studies of Lake Mendota, conducted in concert with Chauncey Juday, served as a foundation for development of the science of limnology in North America.

Robert M. La Follette remains one of Wisconsin's towering political figures. A classmate of Van Hise, he exercised his influence as governor in the appointment of Van Hise as the university's eighth president. Van Hise split with La Follette when he said that La Follette's policies on World War I were "dangerous to the country." This photo shows La Follette speaking on the steps of the state capitol in 1924, the year he ran as a third-party candidate for president of the United States.

The attitude of assurance that comes with years of experience, leadership, and service is apparent in this 1918 photograph of key figures in the university's history. The group comprises, from left to right: President Charles R. Van Hise, former president Thomas C. Chamberlin, Dean of Agriculture Harry L. Russell, former agriculture dean William A. Henry, and Professor Stephen M. Babcock.

This 1914 photo shows the "Regents at Work." At the time, the board consisted of fifteen members, two of whom had to be women. Thirteen were appointed by the governor from each congressional district and at large; one was the state superintendent of public instruction; the president of the university served ex officio. A member of this board, Elizabeth Waters, represented the sixth district from Fond du Lac. She served as a regent on three separate occasions and has since been remembered through the women's dormitory which bears her name.

When President Van Hise died unexpectedly in November 1918 following routine surgery, his funeral was held in the lobby of the University Library on the Lower Campus. This photo shows the forming of the cortege and the loading of the casket for the trip to Forest Hills cemetery.

Correspondence instruction, depicted in this State Fair display, offered another means of university outreach. The audience served through this approach was considered extremely broad, including everyone from "misfits, who having started wrong, desire to change their occupations" to homemakers and professional men.

In 1915 students staged a massive University Exposition held in the Armory and its annex to give "the faculty, the students and the state a 'Birds-eye View of the University.'" The exhibition, which featured displays from virtually every department of the university, drew more than eight thousand people. This ninety-thousand-volt wireless telegraph station demonstrated the possibilities of communicating through thin air. A short time later, the university became a leader in the development of educational broadcasting. Experiments initiated in the physics department eventually led to the establishment of radio station 9XM, later known as WHA, "the oldest station in the nation."

E. L. Luther, Wisconsin's first county agent (serving Oneida County), became the first county agent in the United States to work under a legislative grant. He is shown here in 1912 with the two-cylinder racing motorcycle he used in traveling to his experimental plots and to meetings in town halls and schoolhouses and with individual farmers.

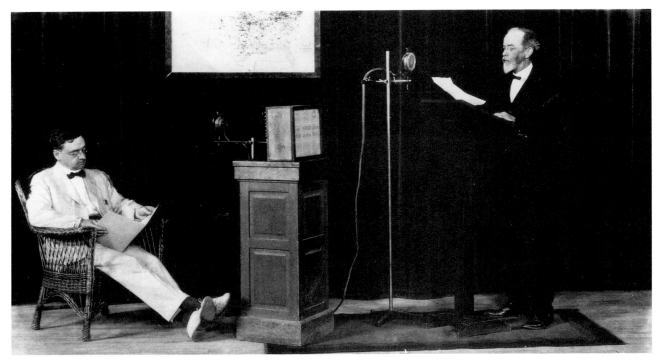

Leaders in the early educational broadcasting experiments were professors F. M. Terry (left) and William H. Lighty, shown here in a broadcast studio in Sterling Hall about 1923.

As the century progressed, technology became more elaborate and complex. The steam and gas engineering laboratory of Professor William Black (left) was "well equipped with a variety of steam and gas engines, specially arranged for experimental work, and for the principles discussed in the classroom."

By the second decade of the
century, the automobile, then
known as the "horseless
carriage," became an increasingly common mode of
transportation. Nevertheless,
horses were still used extensively
on the farm. The College of
Agriculture, through its animal
husbandry program, continued
to maintain a herd of draft
horses for breeding, instruction,
and research purposes.

With agriculture as such an essential part of the Wisconsin economy, the university found ways to serve the diverse segments of the state's farming community. The young people's class shown here is an example: "A week's course of lectures, demonstrations, and exercises in grain growing and judging, selection and testing of seeds and other subjects relating to farm life which are interesting to farm boys and girls."

The horticulture greenhouses have been a familiar part of the campus landscape for several generations. This photo shows an early class setting out plants for study and cultivation.

Charles R. Bardeen, the university's primary exponent of medical education, is shown here in his anatomy laboratory in 1914. The university established the Medical School in 1907, as a two-year program with Bardeen as dean.

The university established the School of Domestic Science during the 1903–1904 academic year following prodding from Belle Case La Follette and others who garnered legislative support for the program. Instruction began in the second semester under the supervision of Professor Caroline Hunt. This photo depicts a 1905 nutrition demonstration. According to an early report from the board of overseers, "This is not a mere 'cooking school,' but from the work done here, Wisconsin cannot fail to get better housekeepers and home makers. The work of the department demands of its students a knowledge of chemistry, dietetics, sanitation, economics, and market values."

Lower Campus development changed the Lake Mendota shoreline, as is evident from this turn-of-the-century photograph, which shows the University Boathouse and Armory with Science Hall and the Chemical Engineering Building immediately beyond.

The Lower Campus emerged as a clear and distinct area with the identification of an open field bounded on the west by Park Street, the north by Langdon Street, and the south by State Street. This photo shows the new Science Hall, constructed on the site of the original structure, which had been gutted by fire in 1884. The homes along Langdon Street included (from left) the residences of President and Mrs. Charles Kendall Adams, John and Helen Olin, George and Frances Raymer, and Professor and Mrs. Edward A. Birge. Olin, a Madison attorney, became a regent and willed his subsequent home at 130 North Prospect Avenue for the official residence of the head of the university. Raymer, part owner and editor of the Madison Argus and Democrat newspaper, served as a regent from 1885 to 1891 and was president of the board in 1890 and 1891.

By 1900 the perimeter of the Lower Campus field had changed significantly, assuming a somewhat imposing character with the addition of the State Historical Society and University Library building, the University YMCA, and the new Armory and Gymnasium.

As the State Historical Society of Wisconsin expanded its activity through the second half of the nineteenth century, pressure developed to find a suitable home for it beyond the quarters occupied in the old state capitol. The legislature appropriated funds in 1893 to construct a new headquarters for the society and to house the expanding collections of the University of Wisconsin Library. The building, a majestic classical structure, opened in 1900. The large reading room of the library, shown here, served university students until the 1950s, when the Memorial Library provided much-needed space for the university's expanded collections. The Historical Library continues to house the American history collection, one of the leading resources of its kind.

The university purchased Camp Randall in 1893 as a site for men's athletics and constructed a grandstand in 1896 for various events. This photo, taken from University Hall about 1900, shows the grandstand, surrounded by a large track, and the playing field which had an east-west orientation. The grandstand was replaced in 1916 by the permanent stadium located at the southwest corner of the site, a move which changed the football field to a north-south orientation.

The connection between the university and the farm continued to grow during the new century. Agriculture Hall was completed and occupied in the fall of 1903. Built with a $150,000 legislative appropriation and an additional $25,000 for fittings, it housed the administrative offices of the college and experiment station, the departments of agronomy, animal husbandry, bacteriology, and chemistry, and the offices of the superintendent of the farmers' institutes.

One of the important cooperative ventures of the Van Hise era was the decision to locate the United States Forest Products Laboratory in Madison. The university built and equipped the lab in 1910; the government provided the scientists who interacted with faculty. When the lab relocated to new quarters on the western edge of the campus in the 1930s, this building became the home of the mining and metallurgical engineering department. This photo also shows the growing development of University Heights in the background.

The Camp Randall Memorial Arch was dedicated in 1912 in remembrance of the seventy thousand troops who had trained on the premises during the Civil War. In 1893 a segment of the land had been designated as a veterans memorial park and the balance conveyed to the university "for military drill and athletic purpose."

The College of Agriculture used the western edge of the campus for farm activities for many years. As Dean William A. Henry noted in 1904, "Indeed it is hard to tell where the campus ends and the farm begins." This photo shows a portion of the dairy herd grazing in the area just west of the present location of Elizabeth Waters Hall.

Always a focal point for activity on the Lower Campus, Lake Mendota provided a site for aquatics instruction, as illustrated in this 1917 photo. The instructor here, Joe Steinhauer, started his university career as an athletic trainer and later coached five different sports, including golf and swimming. Steinhauer became one of the first sports broadcasters in the country, covering university activities for WHA, and also served as Wisconsin state athletic commissioner.

Summer session began to expand in the Van Hise era, as schoolteachers and principals were required to obtain extra academic credits. The university purchased portions of a farm on the shores of Lake Mendota west of Second Point and established a tent colony, shown here in 1915, to provide low-cost summer housing for educators and their families.

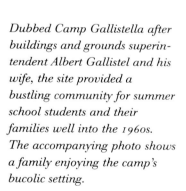

Dubbed Camp Gallistella after buildings and grounds superintendent Albert Gallistel and his wife, the site provided a bustling community for summer school students and their families well into the 1960s. The accompanying photo shows a family enjoying the camp's bucolic setting.

This 1900 photo, taken in the gym of Ladies Hall, shows the women's freshman basketball squad.

VOL. VII   **NO. 11**

Today's concern about overemphasis of intercollegiate athletics is hardly a new phenomenon, as suggested by this cover from a 1906 issue of the Sphinx, *a UW humor magazine. In a speech to the alumni during the same year, Professor Frederick Jackson Turner decried the practice of faculty "certifying the eligibility of mercenaries" who traveled from one institution to another to play for pay. Turner, in a refrain that has echoed from one generation to another, noted, "The public has pushed its influence inside the college walls, and is demoralizing student sentiment, exalting fictitious heroes, and condoning brutality, setting up false ideas of the true honor of a university, and making it impossible for faculties and for the clean and healthy masses of the students to keep athletics honest and rightly related to a sane university life."*

"On, Wisconsin," which became one of the most popular college songs, made its appearance as the university's fight song during the Van Hise era.

The Women's Athletic Association was founded in 1907. Originally formed as a "secret," elective society, it soon opened up to provide ready access to all women students who could meet "the necessary athletic requirements." Students had to participate in various sports, no more than one per semester, to qualify for membership and gain awards ranging from a small emblem to a W sweater. This 1916 photo shows an active moment during an outdoor baseball game. Other women's sports included indoor baseball, field hockey, basketball, bowling, swimming, archery, tennis, and track. The white top with neckerchief became the standard women's sports uniform of the day.

One of the more unusual episodes in UW athletic history took place in 1909, when the Badger baseball team traveled to Japan. Organized by Genkwan Shibata, a 1909 graduate, and financed by contributions from Keio University in Tokyo, the trip was billed as "the longest ever undertaken by a college athletic organization." The Badgers left in August and returned in November, winning five of the nine games they played before an average of twenty thousand enthusiastic spectators. The team's coach, legislative reference librarian Charles McCarthy, subsequently wrote the book which gave a name to the university's newly emerging educational concept: the Wisconsin Idea.

This photo shows the new stadium, where the largest crowd up to that time in Wisconsin football history (more than twenty-two thousand) watched Wisconsin beat Illinois 14–9 on November 13, 1920.

Basketball in the Armory was a popular winter diversion. The 1921 Badger team is shown here in an 18–12 winning effort against Minnesota. The Badgers won consistently throughout the first fifty years of UW basketball history. They finished this season in a three-way tie for first place, sharing the conference title with Michigan and Purdue.

A temporary bleacher collapsed during the second quarter of the Wisconsin-Minnesota football game on November 20, 1915, injuring several students and spectators. The famous sportswriter Ring Lardner was there that day and filed a report, writing in his argot as Al, the sports fan: "They was about 1,000 or maybe about five thousand people in one of the cheering stands and all of a sudden it caved in somewhere and all the people was thrown on the ground. Some of 'em was hurt pretty bad." Volunteers quickly came to the aid of the injured, and those who required hospitalization were released by early the following week. The next season, football games were played in a newly constructed stadium equipped with permanent seats.

During World War I the university instituted a course for training auto mechanics for the United States Army, utilizing the space available in the Stock Pavilion for demonstration and practical application. The course continued as vocational training following the war and was "open to all persons (not regular university students) over eighteen years of age who have completed grammar school work." University students, except freshmen, could take an abbreviated version of the course as an elective.

During the spring of 1918 four hundred soldiers came to the university to receive vocational training in such areas as shop, electrical work, and gas engines. The men were billeted in the Armory and ate their meals in the Armory Annex. Some regular classes were shifted to the evening to accommodate the visitors.

When a large percentage of the men students had gone off to war, women students were called on to pursue instruction in such areas as engineering mechanics.

More than ten thousand people, led by the university corps of cadets, turned out for this Loyalty Parade led on April 6, 1918. Following the parade, Robert McNutt McElroy, a representative of the National Security League and professor at Princeton University, spoke to an assembly of students at the Stock Pavilion. Because of their perceived indifference to his remarks, he subsequently accused them of being "a bunch of damned traitors."

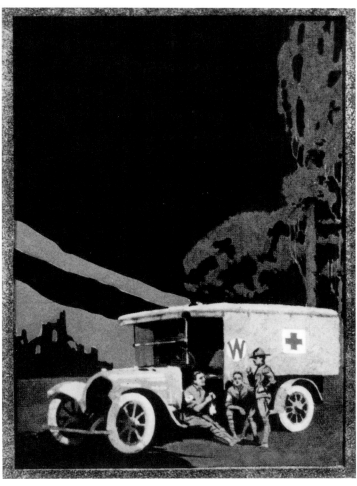

Reactions to McElroy's charges
of disloyalty were substantial
and immediate. On April 26,
students and their supporters
rallied and marched up State
Street and around the square.
They then returned to the
Lower Campus, where they
burned Kaiser Bill and Professor
McElroy in effigy. People were
quick to point out that the university had contributed to the
war effort in numerous and diverse ways. These ranged from
revoking an honorary degree
previously given to the German
ambassador to censuring
Senator La Follette for his
antiwar activity, from providing
more faculty officers for the
military than any other college
or university to establishing the
Student Army Training Corps.
The illustration from the 1919
Badger yearbook provides a
romantic evocation of a group
of former UW students serving
in the Ambulance Corps in
Europe.

The familiar corner of State and Gilman streets forms a vantage point for watching a student parade featuring toga-clad Romans and chariots. The University Co-op, which began its operation here, moved to the northwest corner of the State and Lake street intersection in 1926 and across the street to the present University Book Store site in 1972.

The advent of World War I was accompanied by instruction in military science and tactics as an accepted part of the curriculum. Freshmen and sophomores were required to take the course, while it was an elective for juniors, seniors, and graduate students. This rather bizarre selection for a gun emplacement could be considered acceptable only so long as no one returned the fire.

These illustrations from the Badger *reflect student fashion styles during the early part of the century.*

The Lake Rush, an annual contest of strength between the freshman and sophomore classes, involved a struggle to see who could gain control of a patch of shoreline between the Armory and the University YMCA. Larger incoming classes combined with a growing concern about hazing led to the abolition of the Lake Rush in 1909. It was replaced with the Class Rush.

The Class Rush, which continued the competition between the freshman and sophomore classes, drew thousands of spectators, who ringed the Lower Campus playfield. The purpose of the rush was to capture a series of burlap bags filled with hay and placed in the center of the field. The class with the most bags on its side of the field at the end of fifteen minutes was declared the winner and led a parade up State Street and around the square. Sophomores increased the challenge by kidnapping numbers of freshmen the night before the event. The freshmen were transported out of town, locked in barns or left stranded on lonely country roads, and were consequently forced to find their way back to the campus by various devices to arrive in time for the rush. Both sides had to contend with a quagmire of mud in the center of the field, created by the digging and flooding of shallow trenches in the area.

In addition to its use as a playfield, the Lower Campus also served as an exhibition space, drill field, and the site of various other activities including this trick-riding demonstration held as part of the 1924 Spring Style and Horse Show.

A toboggan slide, located on the slope behind the Washburn Observatory, was a popular source of winter entertainment for many years. Although the slide has been gone for several generations (this photo is from 1911), present-day students sometimes use cafeteria trays from nearby dormitories to propel themselves down the same slope.

In the fall of 1914 a mob of town rowdies armed with clubs attacked and beat some students on the Lower Campus and later in front of the Park Hotel. Student reinforcements assembled, and the group, numbering nearly fifteen hundred, marched up State Street to the square, where the police intercepted them. Four students were arrested and jailed. The mob, pictured here, grew belligerent and stormed the police station. The students were temporarily beaten back with fire hoses. President Van Hise was summoned, and he and Madison mayor Adolf Kayser urged the students to disperse. They did so after Van Hise posted bail for the arrested students.

With the faculty's blessing, a student court handled discipline for most student transgressions, except academic misconduct. The court took its work very seriously, so seriously that it declared, "Failure on the part of a witness to attend a trial when summoned is an offense punishable by contempt of court proceedings from the University."

The activity in editorial offices of student newspapers changes little over the generations. This 1914 photo of Daily Cardinal *staff members shows a rather formally dressed group of budding journalists. The articles of organization adopted that year said that the "paper shall be conducted as an all-university, non-partisan, non-factional paper, for the purpose of presenting all the news of the university in a fair and unbiased manner, of expressing in the editorial columns the best sentiment of the representative student leaders, and of affording an open forum in which all students may express their views within reasonable bounds."*

Looking for an excuse to celebrate during the late winter doldrums, students at the University of Missouri declared in 1903 that St. Patrick was an engineer because of the way he drove the snakes from Ireland. UW engineering students initiated a similar celebration in 1915 and held a parade to mark the occasion. Another professional group—the law students—claimed St. Patrick as their patron saint. This led to decades of claims and counterclaims, which were acted out in a series of events and shenanigans surrounding the annual St. Patrick's Day parade. The photo here shows the engineers assembling for that first parade in 1915.

Students duly celebrated the rites of spring on Bascom Hill for many years beginning early in this century. The events associated with the observances were popular with townspeople and residents of nearby communities—so popular that tickets for seating were sold to make money for the sponsoring organizations. In 1914, May Fete, sponsored by the departments of physical education and home economics, featured a processional showing "spring in various forms by means of Pan and his followers, dryads and wood nymphs, the wind, rain, and waters."

The 1915 program included a picturesque maypole dance and an event honoring graduating women seniors and women students who had outstanding records in scholarship and extracurricular activities. Sponsored by the Women's Self-Government Association, the event became known as Senior Swingout. In addition to showing the pageantry of the event, this picture also depicts an interesting juxtaposition of the domes of the state capitol and University Hall—a symbolic representation of the linkage between the state and the university.

This cover, taken from volume 1 of the campus humor magazine the Wisconsin Octopus, shows the distinctive look of the Roaring Twenties. A popular outlet for campus humor and satire, the Octopus was published for more than three decades.

As described in the 1914 Badger yearbook, "The Junior Prom, first organized in 1896, has become the greatest social event of the year. It is held in the gymnasium and supported largely by fraternities that organize house parties, inviting guests from all sections of the country. It takes place as the chief event of a week of social activity between semesters."

This *1915 sampling of university publications shows the diversity of interests served at the time. The* Daily Cardinal *and the* Wisconsin Daily News *were student newspapers, while the* Wisconsin Magazine, *which absorbed the* Sphinx, *provided an outlet for literary and humorous expression. The* Wisconsin Engineer *and the* Wisconsin Country Magazine *carried news of engineering and agriculture to their respective constituencies, and the* Wisconsin Alumni Magazine *was the principal link between the university and its graduates. According to journalism professor Willard G. Bleyer, "regulation of student publications has been one of* laissez faire, *largely because of an unwillingness on the part of the faculty to interfere with the undergraduates' freedom of utterance. . . . Except in cases of evident violations of good taste and decency practically no censorship has been exercised by faculty or regents."*

The placement of a number of miniature tombstones on Bascom Hill in front of Birge Hall dramatized a worldwide effort to provide famine relief for a 1921 famine in China which affected an estimated fifteen million people.

The Morgan Brothers Cigars and Billiard Hall was a popular State Street hangout during the 1920s. Here William P. ("Dad") Morgan and his brother, David, wait on a customer.

Another campus area attraction of this period was the Schwoegler Candy Company at 528 State Street. Later known as the Chocolate Shop, it proved to be a popular confectionery until the late 1950s.

The Union Vodvil, a popular campus variety show, featured many student acts. Julia Hanks—appearing as a palm-bedecked Cleopatra—took part in an interpretive dance act presented in the 1919 show by the Women's Athletic Association.

The intersection of State and Park streets has always been a busy corner as students come off the hill during class breaks. This scene from the 1920s offers a view of styles of contemporary student dress.

From the Roaring Twenties to World War II

The year 1925 provides an important benchmark to measure the changing nature of the university. The most immediate and tangible manifestation of the university's growing transformation was the appointment of Glenn Frank as president.

At age thirty-seven, Frank became the youngest person ever appointed to the university presidency. He was the first president in the university's history who did not have an earned advanced degree or an established record of service as an educator. His immediate predecessors—Bascom, Chamberlin, Adams, Van Hise, and Birge—had been dedicated scholars before assuming administrative positions. Frank had gained his prominence through utilizing the evangelical fervor he had developed as a young minister to initiate a career as a writer and editor.

He arrived to preside over what had become one of America's preeminent universities. The University of Wisconsin led the nation in the granting of Ph.D.'s in 1925. In the same year one of the university's distinguished faculty members—physicist Max Mason—was named president of the University of Chicago, the Russian historian Alexander Vasiliev came to the university, and Oskar Hagen arrived to establish a program in art history and criticism. Several faculty members published important works in 1925: Max C. Otto in philosophy, William Ellery Leonard in literature, John Lewis Gillin in sociology, and

Margaret H'Doubler in dance. Frederick Paxson received the Pulitzer Prize for his book *History of the American Frontier.*

Faculty research in the life sciences also achieved renown in 1925 as steps were taken to patent a process developed by biochemist Harry Steenbock. Steenbock had discovered that foods irradiated with vitamin D could help eliminate rickets in children. The Quaker Oats Company offered him nine hundred thousand dollars for the exclusive patent rights to his discovery, but he felt that a significant portion of any royalties should be returned to the university to encourage further research.

Others recognized the potential of the idea. Graduate School dean Charles Sumner Slichter, after consulting with Chicago chemist William Hoskins and patent attorney Russell Wiles, advanced the idea of establishing a private foundation to secure and manage the patent. Slichter, Steenbock, Dean of Agriculture Harry L. Russell, UW alumnus and Chicago patent attorney George I. Haight, and Madison attorney Harry Butler put together a charter which established the Wisconsin Alumni Research Foundation (WARF). The trustees were all alumni: Haight, who served as the first president, Madison investor Thomas E. Brittingham, Jr., Madison banker Lucien M. Hanks, Madison attorney Timothy Brown (who would later become a Wisconsin Supreme Court justice), and New York attorney William S. Kies.

The development of WARF and the subsequent stimulation of research funds for university faculty came at the same time the university was spurning funding from private sources. Robert M. La Follette, who had launched a bid for the presidency, no doubt influenced some of this. He questioned the propriety of the university's accepting gifts from millionaires or corporate giants.

La Follette died before he could press the matter further, but the issue surfaced a short time later when the regents accepted a $12,500 grant for medical research from the Rockefeller Foundation. The Madison *Capital Times* labeled the gift "tainted money" and called on the regents to turn back the gift as a repudiation of "interests that are in the business of buying colleges and universities."

While arguments to the contrary came from the faculty, administration, and some elements of the press, the regents reconsidered their original acceptance and adopted a resolution offered by Regent Daniel Grady which said that "no gifts, donations, or subsidies shall in the future be accepted by or on behalf of the University of Wisconsin from any incorporated educational endowments or organizations of like character." The regents' action did not receive broad support. In less than a year they began accepting funds from private sources. By 1930 they rescinded their previous action and subsequently adopted guidelines on the acceptance of gifts. The legislature moved to guarantee objectivity by adopting a resolution which instructed the regents not to accept funds that would obligate the university "to any individual, corporation or organization, or if the gift was designed to promote the sale of commodities or services."

In the meantime, Glenn Frank was busy promoting academic initiatives. Shortly after he arrived at the university, he set the wheels in motion to establish an intensified liberal arts program which became known as the Experimental College. Dr. Alexander Meiklejohn, former president of Amherst College, had advanced the original idea. Meiklejohn discussed his plan in articles published in the *Century* (when Glenn Frank was its editor) and the *New Republic*. He patterned his idea on a classical or European approach featuring small group discussions and tutorial sessions between master and pupil. The new program departed from the utilitarian or vocational orientation that had been evolving for more than a generation.

As a start, Frank appointed Meiklejohn to the faculty, then sought institutional ratification for the program. This he did through the creation of an All-University Commission "to study problems of improvement of instruction and more helpful contacts between students and faculty." The group moved rapidly. In the spring of 1926 it recommended that an Experimental College be established in the College of Letters and Science. In a fortunate coincidence, a new set of men's dormitories were being constructed in the lakeshore area on the western edge of the campus at the time. Adams Hall provided an ideal environment and accommodation for the college.

The concept of the Experimental College went against a trend toward large lecture classes established earlier in the century which continued to hold sway, particularly as university enrollments grew. While the Letters and Science faculty adopted the All-University Commission's recommendation to establish the new program, it did so without apparent enthusiasm. The first classes began in the fall of 1927 with an enrollment of 119 freshmen. While enrollment rose in the second year with the arrival of 91 new freshmen, the program began to decline in the third year and was phased out in 1932 after its advisers recommended termination. Although the Experimental College had little discernible influence beyond the university, it did suggest a model for the Integrated Liberal Studies program which was established in 1949.

Concurrent with the development of the Experimental College, the College of Letters and Science initiated a substantial review of its curriculum in 1929 and 1930 through a committee under the leadership of history professor Carl Russell Fish. The committee's report included a provision that freshmen be given the opportunity to take advanced courses if they could pass attainment examinations. The report also authorized students to take majors in more than one department, tightened foreign language and general requirements, and proposed that no students be admitted to study in their junior year unless they had achieved a minimum grade point average above a *C*.

Accommodation had been made early in Van Hise's administration to the growing size and diversity of the faculty through the establishment of the committee system to deal with important matters of faculty governance. Glenn Frank found this system well established as the way of doing business. He recognized that faculty acceptance was necessary to move any of his programs forward. He and the faculty developed a working relationship that avoided major impasses. In the meantime, Frank continued his previous practice of making speeches in a number of different forums and writing widely syndicated newspaper columns. The faculty went about its business of tending to the academic affairs of the university.

Through the administrations of Van Hise and Birge, the faculty had grown together to form an interlocking structure. Frank tried to displace the department as the principal focus for scholarly activity in a 1930 memo entitled "A Functional Organization of Faculty Forces." It called for the establishment of "institutes" organized by graduate divisions such as social sciences, biological sciences, language and literature, etc. He argued that scholarly inquiry and the diffusion of knowledge was becoming too expansive to be encompassed in the traditional departments. His proposal received a polite hearing at a faculty meeting but no follow-through. Frank's idea reflected recognition of the growing interdependence of the university's academic program. His concept lay dormant until 1942, when faculty divisions in the natural sciences, physical sciences, humanities, and social sciences were established to oversee curricular developments and to advise the deans on the promotion of faculty to tenure.

Besides the formal activities represented by the department and regular faculty meetings, faculty had developed important informal relationships through what former Letters and Science dean Mark Ingraham called "a soviet of dining clubs." As Ingraham observed, "Breaking bread with others does not always lead to agreement but it is perhaps the best road to understanding and develops close friendships." The real business of the faculty, however, was often accomplished at the University Club. A significant number of faculty dined there regularly, and several committees held meetings there each week.

In the 1930s the close-knit social and political relationships of the faculty transferred to the classroom and laboratory. Faculty saw themselves as part of the larger university. A genuine community of scholars, they not only broke bread together but also shared an intellectual curiosity that ranged beyond their respective disciplines. One example of such interaction was Science Inquiry, initiated by geology professor C. K. Leith, biochemist Harry Steenbock, and political scientist Chester Lloyd Jones. The program examined the status of university teaching and research efforts directed toward contemporary social, political, and economic problems. The interchange of ideas produced not only enlightened conversation but also useful bulletins and reports on such topics as game, soil, and water conservation, transportation, public utilities, and crime and delinquency.

Interdepartmental activity also generated a growing awareness of and respect for the natural environment. The mid-1930s saw the addition of two important assets to the University of Wisconsin which advanced its potential as a center for wildlife and conservation study. The first was the appointment of Aldo Leopold as a professor of game management. The second was the transformation of a plot of farmland on the west side of Madison into the University Arboretum. Constructed by a company of workers from the Civilian Conservation Corps who worked on the project from 1935 to 1941, the arboretum re-created the Wisconsin prairie environment as it was around 1840. The establishment of the arboretum led to pioneering studies in plant ecology by such distinguished Wisconsin faculty as John T. Curtis, Henry C. Greene, Norman Fassett, and G. William Longenecker.

In addition to pioneering in environmental studies, the university also moved forward in other areas. John Steuart Curry, the noted regionalist painter from Kansas, was appointed artist-in-residence in the College of Agriculture in 1936. Linked with Grant Wood and Thomas Hart Benton as a celebrator of the midwestern ethos, Curry helped develop the Wisconsin Regional Arts program. Three years later, pianist Gunnar Johansen received a similar appointment in the School of Music.

Change and evolution had been developing on other fronts for a number of years. High jinks and rowdyism characterized many student activities throughout the earlier part of the century. A new perspective emerged in the early 1920s. Hazing was drastically curtailed, and the Varsity Welcome had become a more formal way of introducing newcomers to the university. The new Memorial Union fulfilled an idea advanced in Van Hise's inaugural: he had called for the establishment of a union which "should be a commodious and beautiful building, comfortably, even artistically furnished."

Students were extremely active in providing $1.5 million in funding for the Union. Opened in 1928, the building was "Erected and Dedicated to the Memory of the Men and Women of the University of Wisconsin Who Served in Our Country's Wars." Those memorialized included 218 men and 1 woman; 179 had died in the World War and 30 in the Civil War.

Prior to the Union's construction, fraternities, sororities, and the University YMCA had provided an important focus for student activity. These had limited potential for programming. The new facility, however, provided students with a "home for Wisconsin Spirit," which offered meeting rooms, dining rooms, recreational space, and facilities to accommodate various cultural events. Many events which had been functioning for several years now moved to the Union, including the Union Vodvil, a variety show which had been staged at the Fuller Opera House in downtown Madison; the annual Haresfoot production, an all-male theatrical performance which featured males in female roles; and the Senior Prom. New programs were initiated, including the Hoofer Outing Club; a craft workshop; a music, theater, and film program; and a concert series. As Porter Butts, director of the Union from 1926 to 1967, pointed out, "The Union developed by the mid '30s some 130 types of programs and services . . . which simply didn't exist before."

These developments paralleled the maturing of Glenn Frank's presidency. As his tenure in office lengthened, his boy-wonder image began to lose some of its luster. The relationship between the faculty and the president, polite but never intimate, became more distant in June 1932. Hit by a significant reduction in state operating funds—$1.5 million out of a total $5.2 million in appropriations—the university had to reduce expenditures dramatically in response to the Depression-induced cutbacks. Faculty salaries provided an obvious source for savings. There was general opposition to imposing layoffs or firings, so the regents devised a plan to reduce salaries. The reductions ranged from 20 percent for those in the higher salary brackets to 12 percent for teaching assistants. Frank showed no inclination to set an example of personal commitment to this cause. The level of his salary and benefits remained proportionately high through the period.

Meanwhile, deeper political forces were at work. Although Robert M. La Follette had died in 1925, his spirit and his politics were being carried forward by his sons—Robert, Jr., who assumed his father's seat in the United States Senate, and Philip, who was elected governor of Wisconsin in 1930. The La Follettes and their supporters saw Frank as a symbol of conservative influence.

Other factors began to erode Glenn Frank's position. The most corrosive attack against him came in an article by Ernest L. Meyer, "Glenn Frank: Journalist on Parole," which appeared in the February 1934 issue of the *American Mercury* magazine. Meyer characterized Frank as "a man enthralled by his own eloquence" and claimed that the president had "probably not a single sincere admirer left among the host who hailed his coming with hosannas."

An accumulation of episodes and circumstances had generated doubts about Frank's sincerity and ability. Internal problems raised further questions about the condition of the university and the quality of Frank's leadership. The regents fired Extension Division dean Chester Snell after a regent committee had found his administration to be sloppy and tyrannical. The zealous policing of student morality by Dean of Men Scott H. Goodnight and Dean of Women F. Louise Nardin also created a backlash of criticism. Athletic director Walter E. Meanwell and football coach Clarence W. Spears also were fired. The two had quarreled regularly, and Meanwell was found to be personally profiting from the sale of athletic equipment. Spears, on the other hand, was accused of using improper means to improve the performance of his teams. The drive against Frank was further accelerated after he showed his conservative leanings by openly criticizing Franklin Roosevelt's New Deal policies. His comments came amid increased speculation that he was a possible Republican nominee for president of the United States.

At the beginning of 1936 Governor La Follette appointed five Progressives to the board of regents. These new additions, combined with earlier appointments, gave the governor control of the board. Regent president and Madison attorney Harold M. Wilkie became the principal board exponent of doubts about Frank's ability to successfully administer the university. At the March meeting of the regents, Wilkie suggested that Frank resign for the good of the university. No immediate public response came from the remainder of the board or Frank himself, but considerable maneuvering over Frank's status took place during the ensuing months.

Wilkie and the Progressives continued to press their case, maintaining that their criticisms of Frank involved his management and leadership skills, not his politics. Frank personally defended his record at the December 1936 meeting of the regents and refused to resign. The regents' executive committee subsequently called a special hearing for January 6, 1937. Meanwhile, strong and broad-based support for Frank poured in from across the country, representing support for Frank himself and expressing a deep-seated anxiety about the rising political interference in university affairs and its possible threat to academic freedom. While the rumbling outside the university grew in volume, the faculty generally remained silent. The regents' two-day hearing in early January reviewed allegations about Frank's administrative effectiveness and heard counterarguments by Frank and a number of his adherents, a group which included regents, alumni, and administrators. The board then voted 8–7 that Frank not be reappointed in June and that he be placed on an immediate leave of absence.

Students marched on the governor's office the following day to voice their objections over Frank's dismissal by the board of regents. Governor Philip La Follette declined to intercede, and no one was inclined to reopen the matter. The furor subsided quickly, but a certain bitterness lingered.

Frank got his university affairs in order, continued his writing and lecturing, and later mounted a campaign as a Republican candidate for the United States Senate. The campaign and his career ended tragically on September 15, 1940, when he and his son, Glenn, Jr., were killed in an automobile crash near Greenleaf, Wisconsin.

Any objective evaluation of Frank's twelve-year tenure as president must deal with the very real accomplishments of his administration. While the Experimental College ended after a comparatively short period, it did generate a new excitement for learning and a reminder that education exists to cultivate the mind as much as to prepare students for making a livelihood. Frank also made a number of excellent appointments: the deans of six colleges, a dean of women, and a director of libraries.

Although faculty did not openly rise to Frank's defense, their quality and scholarly productivity remained consistently high during his tenure. Frank also helped revitalize the Farm Short Course, giving it a more direct role in the lives of the state's future farmers. And he fervently defended free speech, speaking out often in the face of criticisms that the university was a kind of ideological compost heap nurturing atheism and communism.

The summary dismissal of Glenn Frank left open wounds in the university's body politic. The regents moved quickly to fill the leadership void. They named Letters and Science dean George Clarke Sellery acting president as they sought a successor. Two months after Frank's ouster they picked Clarence A. Dykstra. Interestingly, Dykstra offered the same academic credentials that Glenn Frank had when he came to the presidency—a bachelor's degree. While Dykstra had taught political science and, like Frank, had picked up honorary degrees, his main experience was with city clubs—those civic advancement groups prominent during the time—in Cleveland, Chicago, and Los Angeles. Immediately before coming to Wisconsin, he had served for seven years as city manager of Cincinnati. In that environment he had successfully balanced civic concerns against political maneuvering.

Dykstra's demeanor and administrative style seemed ideally suited to smoothing things over. The very meaning of his name in Old Dutch—mender of dikes—suggested a spirit of conciliation. Appropriately, no new or protracted controversies arose during his administration. Newly elected governor Julius Heil helped stabilize the university by creating a nine-member board of regents, with members to be appointed on a rotating basis. This made it virtually impossible for a single governor to load up the board with his appointees.

Dykstra's tenure on the campus and his resultant influence was brief and limited. Called to Washington, D.C., in 1940 to head the Selective Service, he spent much of his time fulfilling that responsibility until he resigned from the university in 1944 to accept the position of provost at the University of California at Los Angeles.

Two years before he left the campus, Dykstra evaluated the position of the university under his leadership. He noted that the university, like the rest of society, had weathered the Depression and was on a stronger financial footing than it had been in several years. The accomplishments of the faculty were highly regarded, and the construction of new buildings provided another sign of progress. These included a new women's dormitory, Elizabeth Waters Hall, and a major addition to the Memorial Union—a fully equipped theater done in distinctive art deco. The new theater wing also included a smaller Play Circle Theater, workshops, and game rooms. In addition, the McArdle Memorial Laboratory for Cancer Research and a new biochemistry building were constructed to advance important research in the life sciences.

The decade of the 1940s began with an inkling of change on the student front. One long-standing tradition was modified when engineering students decided to put on an exposition of recent developments in the profession to replace the annual St. Patrick's Day parade. Further changes, however, were shunted aside by the coming of war and the mobilization.

Clarence Dykstra's style and his approach to resolving problems proved particularly beneficial. His competent and understanding administration produced a therapeutic healing following the divisive firing of Glenn Frank.

The idea of a distinctive and integrated design for the Lower Campus gained considerable impetus during the 1920s, as this sketch by Arthur Peabody indicates. The anchor for the development was to be the newly constructed Memorial Union building. The design also included provision for the construction of a music hall, a Vilas Theater, an administration building, an applied arts building, and a boathouse. These functions have since been incorporated into the area in one form or another, although the design and location of the buildings does not precisely duplicate the Peabody plan.

Wisconsin artist Leon Pescheret designed the interiors of the new Memorial Union. In this lithograph Pescheret highlights the distinctive appeal of the building's Italianate style.

This 1937 map of the campus, designed by Marian Newberry, gives a whimsical view of the variety of 1930s collegiate activities and highlights the physical development of the campus.

By 1930 the major outlines of the growing campus were established. Bascom Hill was well developed, and new groupings of buildings appeared to the west, including a cluster of residence halls and the newly built Wisconsin General Hospital, which contained facilities for the Medical School. To the southwest, the engineering campus would soon develop. The construction of the new Field House, combined with Camp Randall Stadium, provided a distinctive focus for intercollegiate athletics.

Born in modest circumstances in Missouri, Glenn Frank nevertheless carefully cultivated the image of a dandy. He often wore spats and was chauffeured to and from work in a Packard limousine and later a Lincoln Continental.

Glenn Frank joined Letters and Science dean George Clarke Sellery in welcoming the freshman class to the campus in September 1925. It was a rare moment of public concordance for the two; Sellery was later considered to be one of Frank's harshest critics on the faculty.

Venetian Night was a popular spring event held sporadically from before the turn of the century into the 1950s. Described as a "night of romance, beauty and splendor," the event was a boating extravaganza. Boats were often elaborately decorated, as were homes along the Lake Mendota shoreline. Canoes and sailboats floated through the waters as fireworks and blinking Japanese lanterns delighted the participants and thousands of spectators. Quite often, though, rain forced the canceling of the event.

A highlight of the beginning of each school year was the Varsity Welcome extended to incoming freshmen. Dean of the Graduate School Charles S. Slichter here gives a welcome to the 1926 freshman class on behalf of the faculty.

Big Man on Campus or Joe College were popular terms used in the 1920s to describe the socially prominent campus leader of the time. This cartoon from the December 1926 Octopus *shows the paraphernalia associated with the role.*

Dining alfresco on Bascom Hill added a special touch to the spring 1923 Mortar Board supper honoring senior women.

The Experimental College, led by Professor Alexander Meiklejohn, was an educational innovation initiated by Glenn Frank shortly after he became president. Students in the program lived in a separate dormitory in the new Adams Hall on the lakeshore. They were identified by distinctive blazers which featured the owl of Athena on the breast pocket.

Even though students were hard hit by the Depression, typical collegiate activities continued, as this John Groth illustration from the 1931 Badger indicates.

Wisconsin High School, a laboratory school for teacher training, had been a fixture of the campus since 1911. Facilities for observation and directed teaching allowed for the instruction of both the younger students and their teachers.

Students protested against racial discrimination in 1935 outside the Loraine Hotel. The hotel refused to accommodate Negro members of the traveling cast of Marc Connelly's play Green Pastures.

This late 1920s photo reflects increased interest in chemistry training and research, showing the chemistry laboratory with its extensive network of ventilating hoods.

Although the university had a broad base in the sciences, from 1907 it offered only a two-year course in premedicine. Potential doctors had to go elsewhere to receive their degrees. In 1925, however, the Medical School was authorized to grant the *M.D. degree. This photo shows a sampling of the medical instruments used by the fledgling doctors.*

Harry Steenbock, a Wisconsin
native and agricultural chemist,
was one of Wisconsin's giants in
science. He discovered that
foods could be supplied with
vitamin D through irradiation
with ultraviolet light, thereby
eliminating such disabling
diseases as bone-softening
rickets. This Aaron Bohrod
portrait shows Steenbock
surrounded by symbols which
represent his many scientific
accomplishments.

Dr. Walter E. Meanwell, Wisconsin's most successful basketball coach, established a twenty-season record of 246 victories and 99 defeats. His teams won eight Big Ten championships and finished second four times. His Meanwell System was an innovative and much-imitated way of advancing the ball up the court through a series of short passes and blocks. Always a colorful figure, Meanwell was relieved of his duties as athletic director in 1936 after an extended period of squabbling with football coach Clarence W. ("Doc") Spears.

Economist John R. Commons came to the university as a protégé of Richard T. Ely. During a career of teaching and research that spanned thirty years, Commons established Wisconsin as one of the major centers for the study of labor history. He also contributed to the Wisconsin Progressive tradition through a close association with Robert M. La Follette. Commons was the principal architect of legislation which established a merit civil service system for the state and the Wisconsin Industrial Commission. He was a leading influence in the development of standards for workmen's compensation, maximum hours, minimum wages, and employers' liability.

Lucky Lindy—Charles A. Lindbergh—was an international celebrity following the first solo flight across the Atlantic from New York to Paris in 1927. Lindbergh had been a student in the College of Engineering from 1920 to 1922. When he visited Madison to receive an honorary LL.D. degree in 1928, he was the guest of President and Mrs. Frank and joined in reunion activities with the members of the class of 1924. He is shown here speaking at the University Convocation.

Scott H. Goodnight, the university's first dean of men, served in the position for twenty-nine years, from 1916 to 1945. An often controversial figure, he was noted for strict discipline in his efforts to extend the university's influence to the off-campus lives of the students. One such incident occurred in

1929. The dean camped briefly on a rocking chair on a sleeping porch at an apartment near the campus as he waited to confront two students—a man and a woman—who had apparently spent the night together. The students were subsequently expelled, and the rocking chair incident became a part of

campus legend. Dean Goodnight's counterpart, both in function and spirit, was F. Louise Nardin, who served as dean of women from 1918 to 1931.

Philosophy professor Max C. Otto was one of the university's most popular teachers during his thirty-six years as a faculty member. His course Man and Nature dealt with theology and evolution from a controversial point of view. Those who preferred a more orthodox approach to questions about the function of business and the existence of God were unsettled by Otto's teaching. Students, however, clamored to get into his class, and the administration consistently supported him throughout his career.

Professor Benjamin ("Benny") Snow was popularly known as the Snow Flake Man for his study of the physical properties of snowflakes. His enthusiasm and creativity in inventing devices to demonstrate the physical properties of matter made his lectures and demonstrations in the principles of elementary physics enormously popular. He is shown here with a special contraption he fashioned to produce a man-made geyser.

Aldo Leopold became the first professor of game management at the University of Wisconsin in 1933. His position, supported by a grant from the Wisconsin Alumni Research Foundation, led to the establishment of what is now the Department of Wildlife Ecology. Leopold helped establish the University Arboretum and served as its first research director. His books, Game Management *and* A Sand County Almanac, *remain basic texts for the practical and aesthetic consideration of* preserving the natural environment. Leopold's concept of the "land ethic" continues to serve as the golden rule of natural resource management and preservation.

Aldo Leopold worked closely with Byron Jorns, bulletin illustrator for the College of Agriculture. Jorns's illustrations, such as the pheasant in the field, were used in pamphlets *that Leopold prepared on wildlife topics. Jorns also did watercolors of campus and state scenes. His depiction of the Poultry Building at 1800* *University Avenue (now the home of the Sea Grant Institute) and the chicken coops in the background exemplifies the documentary record he created.*

G. William Longenecker, also instrumental in the design and development of the arboretum, served as its executive director from 1932 to his retirement in 1966. Longenecker, a landscape architect, helped found a department in his discipline at the university.

The University Arboretum was developed in the 1930s. One of the appealing aspects of this nature preserve and botanical study area is the duck pond along Nakoma Road. The site, of approximately thirty-two acres, provided through the cooperation of the Madison Realty Company, includes a natural spring framed on its west side by stonework reportedly designed by Frank Lloyd Wright.

A group of workers from the Civilian Conservation Corps, a federal public works agency established during the Depression, carried out the major construction of the arboretum. The workers lived at "Camp Madison" in the central portion of the tract. Some of the buildings still remain in the arboretum's administrative area.

Regionalist painter John Steuart Curry became artist-in-residence at the university in 1936. He is pictured here in a Life *magazine article with his famous portrait of the abolitionist John Brown in the background. A horse show at the university's Stock Pavilion inspired his painting* Belgian Stallions.

The university continued and expanded its work in agricultural and cooperative extension during the 1930s. One important component of the program was the work of county home demonstration agents, whose ability to reach families was enhanced by the automobile. In the photo below, Wood County agent H. R. Lathrope demonstrates a tree-planting machine. Field demonstration plots and the campus greenhouses, which provided facilities for studies and experiments in plant pathology and plant breeding, represent additional extension activities.

Iowa-born artist Grant Wood, a contemporary of John Steuart Curry's, received an honorary degree in 1936 and subsequently created this lithograph to commemorate the event. Wood's biographer, UW art historian James Dennis, points out that Wood "could not resist the temptation to poke fun at the affected solemnity of the ritualized custom."

During the 1930s lower Langdon Street became a principal boarding point for intercity bus travel. This scene shows two buses waiting to load passengers in front of the Memorial Union. Fifty years later the scene repeated itself, as buses for Chicago and O'Hare International Airport arrived and departed several times daily.

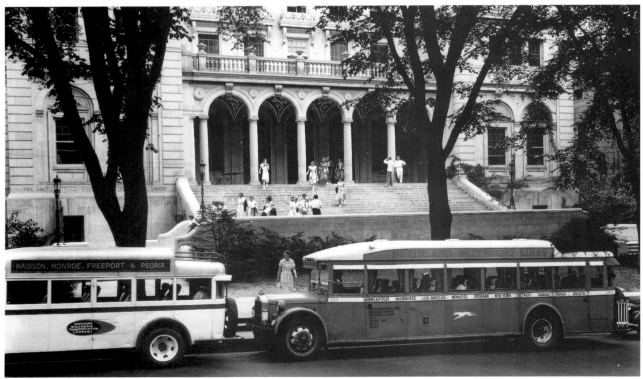

Glenn Frank appeared before the regents during a two-day hearing early in January 1937 to unsuccessfully defend his record as president. The regents voted 8–7 that his appointment not be renewed.

Following Frank's dismissal, students marched on the capitol to voice their objections to Governor Philip La Follette (left). The governor refused to take any action, and the furor soon subsided.

The career of Glenn Frank ended tragically on September 15, 1940. He and his son, Glenn, Jr., were killed in an automobile accident fifteen miles south of Green Bay as they hurried to meet a speaking appointment connected with Frank's campaign for the Republican nomination for the United States Senate.

The Wisconsin Union Theater, designed by Michael M. Hare in consultation with Lee Simonson, was dedicated in 1939. The New York Times called the new facility "one of the finest legitimate theatres in America." Wisconsin native Alfred Lunt and his wife, Lynn Fontanne, among America's most celebrated theater couples, appeared in the inaugural production, The Taming of the Shrew.

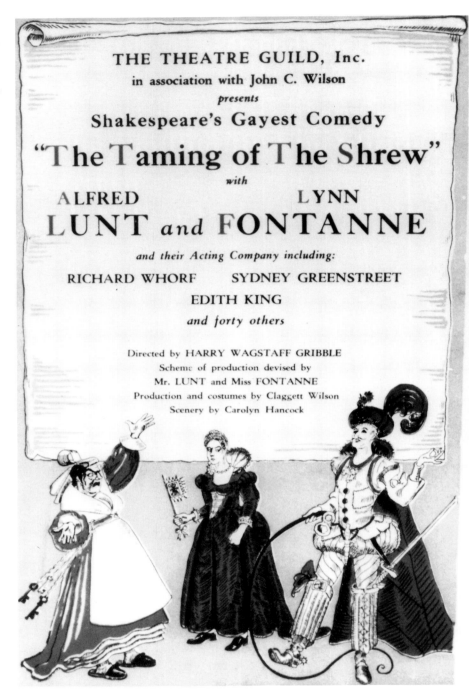

A Contemporary Portfolio

The university is always changing. Some elements from the past carry forward. Others are frozen in time and eventually disappear from memory. The most common and tangible evidence of continuity is the physical domain of the campus—the landscape, the buildings, the technical apparatus of research and scholarship. Less immediately apparent, less easy to capture from a visual perspective, are the ideas and attitudes that weave their way through the university's history.

The major portion of this book describes and depicts the various periods of university development. Ideas and issues are folded into the text and the captions. The narrative itself concludes at the end of the 1970s, a logical breaking-point. And yet life at the university goes on.

This color portfolio is a sampling of images from the 1980s, postcards which speak to the presence of tradition as they capture new developments. While it is too early to impose a detached perspective on this period, the images give a hint of the history that is being shaped by various events and activities.

The pedestrian overpass forms a gateway to Bascom Hill over North Park Street.

Music Hall seen in a moment of winter serenity.

This stained-glass window panel in Music Hall is a colorful architectural embellishment from the nineteenth century.

The picturesque slope west of Elizabeth Waters Dormitory has long been a favorite campus vista.

Chancellor Donna E. Shalala carries forward the precepts of the Wisconsin Idea, which extend back more than a century to the administration of John Bascom.

Commencement provides an opportunity for medieval pageantry as well as creating a sense of proud achievement for the graduates.

Sailboating on Lake Mendota is a perennially favorite sport for members of the Hoofer Sailing Club.

Feeding the ducks on the lakeshore at the Memorial Union provides a momentary diversion from academic concerns.

Study and relaxation go hand-in-hand on the Memorial Union Terrace.

A summertime sunset over the Hoofers' pier.

The plaza at Helen C. White Hall.

A temporary installation of banners on Bascom Hall adds color and pageantry to the everyday scene.

The outdoor classroom is a familiar aspect of fall and spring on the campus.

A walk or ride along the campus lake path is a pleasant seasonal activity.

This telescope in Washburn Observatory has been in service for more than a century.

Practice for the women's crew takes place against the backdrop of the campus skyline.

Flowering crabapple trees herald the coming of spring on the Library Mall.

The galleries of the Elvehjem Museum of Art provide space for displays of exhibitions and works from the permanent collection.

Flowers and architecture lend a distinctive dignity to Henry Mall.

The Clinical Science Center on the western end of the campus.

The atrium at University Hospital and Clinics in the Clinical Science Center offers an interesting example of contemporary campus architecture.

The plaza at the western end of the computer science complex provides an interesting pattern when viewed from above.

Football and fun are the staple of fall afternoons at Camp Randall Stadium as band director Mike Leckrone sets the tone for halftime and postgame entertainment.

Neon snakes on Lincoln Terrace reflect the sense of play that is a continuing feature of campus life.

South African Archbishop Desmond Tutu spreads a message of international goodwill at the Field House. On a separate occasion, demonstrators press the point that the struggle against apartheid continues.

Students find various means to enhance learning and self-expression in the studio, classroom, and laboratory.

Plant pathologist Paul Williams and chemist Bassam Z. Shakhashiri are recognized for their efforts to stimulate interest in science education.

The College of Agriculture dairy herd is a major source of study for development in one of the state's principal industries.

The ice cream at Babcock Hall is a tantalizing by-product of the university's food science program.

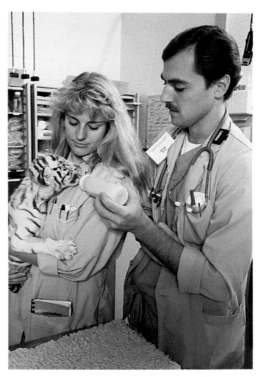

During the 1980s, the newly established School of Veterinary Medicine offered a broad range of training to prepare students for the profession.

Although change is a fact of campus life, the need to study remains constant from one student generation to the next.

Members of Los Hermanos Avilas perform an Aztec dance at the annual multicultural orientation reception.

Suzy Favor, one of the UW's most consistently successful athletes, dominated middle distance running during her four-year career in the late 1980s.

The Badger hockey team won five national championships within twenty years, most recently at Detroit in 1990.

This aerial view shows the expanse of the contemporary campus.

Beginning
a Second
Century

Shortly after Clarence A. Dykstra became president in 1937, the university joined the nation in preparing for a war that would tap its resources and set its program priorities for an entire decade. Mobilization was apparent in a number of ways. Following the Japanese attack on Pearl Harbor, university enrollment declined significantly as a generation went off to fight. At the beginning of the 1940–1941 academic year, 11,376 students were on campus; 3,720 of that total were women. By 1944–1945, enrollment had dropped to 6,615, with 4,531 women.

The campus resembled a military camp, as it was transformed into a training station for various programs. For the first time, women made up a portion of the military delegation. They had become an integral part of the armed forces as each branch of the service established a women's auxiliary for service in noncombat assignments. Schools established on campus for the navy included a radio school, radio training for Waves (the navy women's auxiliary), a school for cooks and bakers, training for navy air pilots, and diesel engineering instruction for naval officers. The army was represented with meteorological training and the training of air force machinists in the mechanical engineering department. In addition, the university ROTC organized the first ski patrol in the nation.

The Alumni Association contributed to the effort of keeping servicemen and servicewomen informed about the university, providing free subscriptions to the *Wisconsin Alumnus* magazine. Students became involved in patriotic activity through blood drives and the collection of scrap metal. Madison became the headquarters of the United States Armed Forces Institute (USAFI). Established in 1941, USAFI utilized the expertise of many university faculty who helped develop correspondence courses for the far-flung servicemen and servicewomen unable to pursue their studies in the traditional classroom or laboratory setting.

The war was winding down in 1945 as the regents selected Edwin Broun Fred to replace Dykstra. A southern patrician and a champion of the sciences, Fred had been a member of the faculty since 1913. He fully understood the university's commitment to faculty governance and the importance of the Wisconsin Idea. His most immediate concern, however, involved dealing rapidly with the postwar pressures placed on the university. The G.I. Bill gave veterans access to higher education in overwhelming numbers, and enrollment more than doubled in 1946–1947, reaching 18,598.

A major housing shortage—for both students and faculty—accompanied the return of the veterans. The regents and the administration prepared for this sudden and substantial demand on the university's physical resources by establishing the Campus Planning Commission. The commission's most pressing concern was finding adequate classroom space and housing.

The university took extraordinary measures and adopted expedient arrangements, both near and well beyond the campus. A significant percentage of the veterans were married; some had or were soon to have children. The military housing that had been a part of the Truax Field Air Base at the northeastern edge of Madison provided housing for 1,500 single students and 100 married couples without children. Badger Village, a part of the sprawling Badger Ordnance Works just south of Baraboo, provided housing for 955 single veterans and 463 married couples.

On campus, trailers appeared on the grounds of Camp Randall, the former Civil War encampment. Virtually all available housing facilities in the greater Madison area became potential student quarters. This included apartments created in Olin House, the official residence of the university president at 130 North Prospect Avenue. The housing problem reflected a similar need for increased classroom space, a situation requiring creative solutions. Quonset huts were constructed on the Lower Campus. Temporary buildings scattered throughout the campus provided classroom and office space that continued in use well into the 1960s. In addition, faculty taught some classes in local churches to utilize every practical form of space.

Aside from the impact of their sheer numbers, the returning veterans had another, more profound influence. They were not interested in the customary sophomoric antics that periodically characterized undergraduate campus life. They had to make up for lost time, to get through the university and into the work force as rapidly as possible. As a result, they concentrated on their studies and got better grades. They precipitated curriculum changes by demanding professional courses that would make the transition from college to the business world smoother and more direct. Finally, they did not hesitate to insist that the university respond to their social and recreational needs.

The Memorial Union became the focal point for student activities. It served as a major social and cultural center, the place to come for dances, music programs, film, and theater and to rent art works. As the "living room of the campus," the Union offered a prime spot for relaxation and recreation, a place where students could come for an interlude between classes or to seek relaxation at the end of the day. It also continued to provide inexpensive and wholesome meals.

The returning veterans brought change to the university's physical, administrative, and academic landscape as the role of the president changed to reflect new realities. E. B. Fred became the chief executive officer of a growing corporate enterprise as he served as the university's chief academic and administrative official. The increasing size and complexity of the university had given it a self-generated momentum. It became an institution that had to be steered rather than consciously propelled forward. Authority had to be delegated. A growing cadre of skilled middle managers shared administrative initiative and responsibility for various activities. Their "branch offices" provided crucial support services but were not immediately involved in instruction or research. These positions included those of the registrar, business manager, secretary of the faculty, director of admissions, dean of men, dean of women, and the directors of the physical plant, University Housing, the Memorial Union, and intercollegiate athletics. Meanwhile, faculty continued their leadership in shaping the academic policy of the institution.

Larger enrollment and a broadening of academic activity increased the need for new facilities. The university desperately needed a new library. Collections had increased dramatically, and the space in the State Historical Society Building, which had housed the university library for nearly fifty years, offered no potential for expansion. Fred, echoing earlier pleas, continually emphasized the need for a new building and pushed to have it placed high on the state building priorities. His persistence produced results. Ground was broken for the Memorial Library in 1950, and it opened in 1953. As the university and the nation began to emerge from the Depression, certain new approaches to education became apparent. These represented both a refinement and a redefinition of the Wisconsin Idea. The university began to reach out to the state in ways that had not been previously possible. Technology provided new vehicles for bringing education to varying constituencies. University extension activities that served traditional agricultural interests had increased in the 1930s. WHA, the university's radio station, provided expanded educational programming under the leadership of Harold B. McCarty and Harold Engel.

While broadcasting continued to have an influence throughout the war, correspondence instruction assumed increased importance as a way of developing and reaching students. Initially, servicemen and servicewomen formed the major portion of students taking correspondence instruction. Later enrollees were Wisconsin citizens who sought personal enrichment or professional upgrading through the mails.

Immediately following the war, the university established thirty-four two-year centers at various locations in Wisconsin. This action literally extended the campus throughout the state. The centers helped respond to the postwar enrollment surge and offered educational and cultural opportunities to local citizens. The postwar university curriculum focused primarily on meeting the veterans' needs by moving students through their studies as quickly as possible. At the same time, alternatives to a standardized program were developed.

Despite all the postwar flurry, there was still time for self-evaluation. A twenty-six-person Committee on University Functions and Policies undertook a detailed look at the university. The group of faculty and administrators, headed by Letters and Science dean Mark Ingraham, presented a twenty-two-page report in December 1949 that offered a new definition of the purpose of the university. It pointed to the growing diversity of the student body and advocated closer ties with the larger society. The major function of the university, the committee said, was "to train the individual to earn a living in a socially useful manner, to develop in him the highest cultural and intellectual interests, and to make him a moral, intelligent and well-informed citizen with a deep sense of obligation to the community."

Much work obviously needed to be done to achieve such a high purpose. Overall, the university was considered good at vocational training but poor in cultural education. The committee made no specific recommendations to address this latter shortcoming. It did, however, reinforce the idea that a principal purpose of the university should be to train people to make a living. To this end, the report advocated creating a central employment service.

The committee found the university's physical plant "deplorably inadequate" and called for improvement in the quality of teaching and in the standing of some academic departments. The age-old and universal problem of cheating on exams elicited concern, as did the need for more effective student advising. In addition, the committee felt that students should be encouraged to take a more active role in self-determination. They should be allowed to sit on committees which dealt with student affairs directly or indirectly.

Finally, considering alumni as a measure of the university's effectiveness, the report noted that UW graduates "often reflect rather than set the ethical tone of their communities." This could be corrected through a more intellectual approach to alumni activities, including meetings "to discuss problems of state, national, or international import, or developments in various fields of knowledge."

The Ingraham committee study came forward in the context of a total review of the university's first hundred years, part of the centennial celebration observed during the 1948–1949 academic year. Preparations for the centennial had begun earlier. In a move similar to the one which established the Wisconsin Alumni Research Foundation twenty years earlier, a group of alumni and friends created the University of Wisconsin Foundation in 1945. Initially called the Gifts and Bequests Council, the new organization had a principal goal of raising five million dollars in time for the centennial observance. Howard I. Potter, an alumnus and Chicago insurance executive, spearheaded the activity as president, and Chicago attorney William J. Hagenah became executive secretary. Another major participant, George I. Haight, had also been closely involved twenty years earlier in the establishment of the Wisconsin Alumni Research Foundation.

The foundation had a purpose beyond the need to raise funds for the centennial. It was becoming obvious that legislative appropriations could not keep up with the increasing needs of the university. The UW Foundation indicated that it would seek gifts and bequests to purchase new equipment, provide fellowships for research, and create scholarships for deserving students.

Meanwhile, the centennial provided the opportunity to evaluate and review ways in which the university had grown and changed during its first century. Since this anniversary coincided with the state's centennial, it also provided a logical opportunity to examine how the university and the state had forged an important partnership through their first hundred years.

The centennial took as its theme a slogan that had originated with Edward A. Birge: "Rooted in the past, serving the present, forming the future." Special displays at the State Centennial Exposition, held at State Fair Park outside Milwaukee, commemorated the role of the university in the life of the state. A film produced by the university's Bureau of Audio-Visual Instruction further underscored the theme. So did the publication of the two-volume *The University of Wisconsin: A History, 1848–1925*, written by Merle Curti and Vernon Carstensen, two distinguished members of the history faculty.

The centennial also provided an opportunity to consider the major issues of the day and the possibilities for the future. Sixteen academic symposia held throughout the year provided "a stimulus to Wisconsin scholarship and research." Scholars from around the country came to the campus to discuss a range of issues. A National Educational Conference attracted 479 delegates from 204 different institutions to review a number of topics related to contemporary higher education. Eleven learned societies held meetings on campus during the year.

Additionally, the centennial highlighted the idea that the university should be a principal center of cultural activity. Famous concert artists performed on campus, including violinist Fritz Kreisler, cellist Gregor Piatigorsky, pianist Vladimir Horowitz, and Leopold Stokowski leading the New York Philharmonic Orchestra. Actors Alfred Lunt and Lynn Fontanne, who had helped dedicate the Union Theater a decade earlier, returned to do a new play, *I Know My Love*. A loaned exhibit of Old Masters from the New York Metropolitan Museum of Art, displayed at the Memorial Union, brought a sampling of world-class art to the university.

The major event of the special centennial observances came in February 1949 with a coast-to-coast Mutual Network radio broadcast of the birthday party. The celebration concluded in June with Commencement-Reunion Weekend. More than ninety thousand alumni, faculty, students, and friends received invitations to the Centennial Dinner, which served as centerpiece for the weekend.

Once again the university reflected the nation, as it poised on the rim of another period of change. The Depression and World War II had created major shifts in the country's political and economic environment. These would subsequently have a profound impact on the shape and content of American higher education. The G.I. Bill made a college education available to an entire generation who otherwise would not have had the opportunity.

President Clarence A. Dykstra brought a relaxed, professional approach to the administration of the university. He is shown here leading the singing at the annual Christmas party held at the president's residence, 130 North Prospect Avenue.

Sinclair Lewis visited the campus in the fall of 1940 as a "professional lecturer in English." He came to the campus to write and stimulate interest in creative writing, but his visit was brief. He left for New York after a four-week stay to initiate an unsuccessful attempt to have his play Felicia Speaking *produced.*

This John Steuart Curry painting, which hangs in the National W Club room, memorializes one of Wisconsin's All-American football heroes, David Nathan Schreiner. Schreiner was killed on Okinawa by Japanese sniper fire during the waning months of World War II.

A high point of Badger athletics occurred when the Wisconsin basketball team beat Washington State 39–34 at Kansas City to win the 1940–1941 National Collegiate Athletic Association championship. Here Coach Harold E. ("Bud") Foster is carried off the floor by team members following the climax of the championship game.

This photo shows the con-
tinuing involvement of students
in the development of the
University Arboretum. Students
organized a Work Day in May
1943 to help plant trees in the
portion of the arboretum south
of what is the present West
Beltline Highway.

World War II brought a prolonged encampment of military personnel on the campus, as the university trained officer candidates through the Navy V–12 program and the Army Specialized Training Program. This photo shows a platoon of future navy officers marching off Bascom Hill to their quarters in the Lakeshore dormitories after attending class.

*This delegation of Waves
marches around the Capitol
Square.*

Correspondence courses developed by the university extension program and often administered through the United States Armed Forces Institute (USAFI) carried the campus to troops abroad. This 1942 cartoon indicates that the overseas environment was not always conducive to concentrated study.

As the war progressed, its tragic toll in human terms became obvious, as reflected in this casualty list displayed at the Memorial Union.

The Kiekhofer Wall in the 600-block of Langdon Street served as a popular campus billboard for nearly twenty years. Originally constructed in 1884 to mark the rear of the property owned by Professor Edward T. Owen, the wall measured 120 feet in length and stood 8 feet high. The custom of painting the wall with student announcements began in 1925 and continued into the late 1940s, when the wall was demolished to provide the way for the eventual construction of the Hillel Center. The wall honored the popular economics professor William Kiekhofer, who managed the property. The scene here is from World War II, when the university provided training for the Navy V–12 program.

This aerial view shows the campus immediately following the war. After a period of little growth, the board of regents approved a plan for twelve new buildings and additions to existing structures. Most were scheduled for the agricultural campus, but a new library and an addition to Wisconsin General Hospital received a high priority.

The return of the veterans following the war placed enormous housing pressures on the community. One response was to convert a portion of the Camp Randall landscape to a trailer camp. Eventually 190 government-surplus trailers provided temporary housing for veterans and their families.

The Civil War cannon evoked memories of a time nearly a century earlier when Camp

Randall was a training ground for Union troops and also served

as a prison for captured Confederate soldiers.

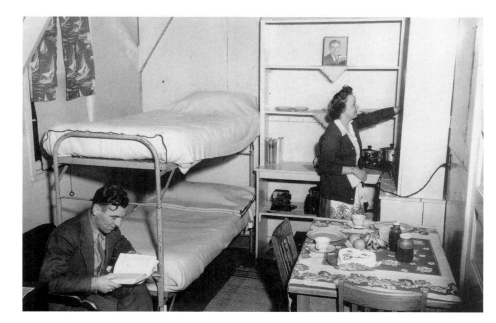

Veterans living in the Camp Randall trailer camp paid twenty-five dollars per month for the spartan quarters which had the familiar look of a military barracks.

The postwar student housing shortage was so acute that the university had to find accommodations wherever possible. Housing originally constructed for government workers at the Badger Ordnance Works south of Baraboo became a thriving student community called Badger Village. The village had its own post office, fire department, grocery store, community building, barber shop, and elementary school. Students made the daily round-trip commute to campus on special buses.

The campus housing shortage generated a new burst of activity at the UW tent colony.

Mr. and Mrs. Charles E. A. Moore are shown studying in a corner of their summer accommodations on the bluff below Eagle Heights.

The pressures of record enrollment following World War II substantially changed the face of the Lower Campus with the addition of seven Quonset huts on the former playfield in the fall of 1946.

The huts provided additional classroom space as well as a reading room for the library. The huts also served as convenient billboards for advertising campus events and activities.

The postwar enrollment pressure is obvious here, as business professor Fayette E. Elwell lectures to a standing-room-only crowd.

Another aspect of the UW participation in the war was the university's cooperation with USAFI. Here, President E. B.

Fred walks with General Omar Bradley and an aide in 1948 on their way to inspect the USAFI headquarters just off the Capitol

Square. General Bradley received an honorary degree during his visit.

Not everyone was convinced of the need for a standing army following World War II. This group of protesters expressed their opposition to the draft during a rally held in December 1945.

Change came to the Memorial Union Rathskeller in late 1941, when the Union directorate approved that the "Men only" sign be removed and women be admitted to the previously all-male sanctuary. One thing that did not change was the bohemian atmosphere that has characterized the Rathskeller from its beginning.

Synchronized swimming and water ballet were popular activities of the Badger Dolphins, the women's honorary swimming club. This stellar formation appeared as part of the 1948 Spring Water Pageant held in the Lathrop Hall pool.

The Homecoming bonfire on the Lower Campus was a major tradition through the 1940s. Wood and used furniture were collected for several weeks before the event, and the ultimate bonfire took on all the *trappings of a pagan ritual, generating enthusiasm for the big game the following day.*

Students have always enjoyed visits to the campus by celebrities. Popular baritone Vaughn Monroe entertained at the first prom held following the war.

Men from Phi Delta Theta fraternity welcomed film star Esther Williams, who was in Madison to promote one of her musical and aquatic film extravaganzas during the late 1940s.

*Beloved music educator Edgar
("Pop") Gordon continued
bringing the joy of music to
schoolchildren through his
broadcasts over WHA radio
even after he formally retired in
the mid-1940s.*

The university's Bureau of Audio-Visual Instruction increased its outreach activities significantly in the late 1940s, as it provided "education on wheels." At the time, the bureau mailed an average of three hundred films per day to Wisconsin grade schools, high schools, and adult groups in five hundred communities around the state.

UNIVERSITY OF WISCONSIN

Centennial

Birthday Party

The university's centennial provided an opportunity to call attention to the teaching, research, and service accomplishments of a century. This program cover is from one of the highlight events of the year-long celebration.

Known across the campus as an iconoclast, Karl Paul Link was a brilliant biochemist who oversaw development of two important discoveries while a faculty member. Dicumarol prevented blood-clotting following surgery. The rodenticide Warfarin, a derivative of dicumarol, was patented and marketed by the Wisconsin Alumni Research Foundation. Income from the patent provided considerable revenue over the years to support additional research on the campus.

In November 1949 the prime minister of India—Pandit Jawaharlal Nehru—visited Madison as part of a goodwill tour of the United States. Nehru, a personal friend of university professor Philo Buck, spoke on the need for world peace and understanding to a capacity audience in the Union Theater. He subsequently greeted another four thousand spectators who had assembled on the Union Terrace in enthusiastic response to his visit.

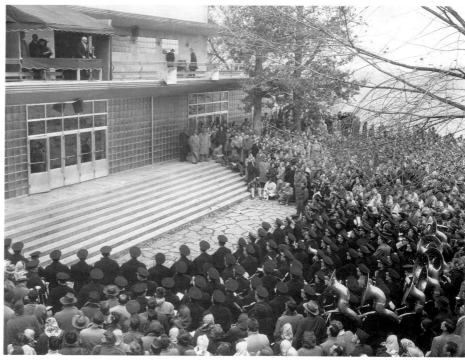

Through the first half of the twentieth century, the Lake Street boundary of the Lower Campus mall was fringed with a block of private homes. The appearance of the area changed considerably after 1950, with construction of the Memorial Library. The library's ground-breaking was a democratic affair. As the planning committee explained: "So many people had a hand in planning the library; every taxpayer of Wisconsin will help pay for it . . . and they all have the right to dig the first shovelful of earth." Included among the early diggers were, from left: university president E. B. Fred; regent president Daniel Grady; Fred V. Platz, Jr., a youngster from the neighborhood who later became a university student; and regent W. J. Campbell.

A temporary delay in the construction of the new Memorial Library occurred in March 1951, when a substantial portion of the steel superstructure collapsed after being hit by the boom of a crane. Fortunately, no one was hurt in the accident.

Chicago artist Aaron Bohrod returned from World War II service with the war art unit in the South Pacific to assume the position of artist-in-residence previously held by John Steuart Curry. Bohrod, who became known for his style of "magic realism," held the position for twenty-five years.

The
Rise
of the
Multiversity

By 1950 a major share of the World War II veterans had completed their education and moved on. The mix of the student population returned to a more traditional age and sex distribution. Yet the beginning of the decade found the United States involved in another armed conflict. This time it was in Korea, a land halfway around the world. Few Americans had ever heard of Korea, and even fewer could locate it on a map.

Although the new outbreak of fighting was unexpected, the nation and the university remained in a state of relative preparedness. Able-bodied male students coming to the university had to enroll in two years of compulsory ROTC. After that they could take two additional years of ROTC, which would lead to a commission and a period of active service, or take their chances on a semester-to-semester draft deferment. This situation created a campus mood of concerned uncertainty. Sporadic protests against ROTC and militarism were counterpoised by outbursts of traditional campus frivolity.

Panty raids started out the decade, as men students made incursions into women's dormitories or sorority houses in search of undergarments. These were followed by water fights and later by contests designed to see how many individuals could be stuffed into a telephone booth. The Wisconsin football team's first appearance in the Rose Bowl in 1953 caused a flurry of excitement, as students followed the team to Pasadena.

Coach Ivan Williamson led Wisconsin football during its most successful run of competition in the modern era. From 1949 to 1955 his teams posted a .674 winning record, including a Big Ten championship and the 1953 Rose Bowl appearance. Enthusiasm generated by the Badger gridiron success led to a 10,000-seat increase in Camp Randall Stadium in 1958, bringing the capacity to 63,710. Additional enthusiasm for Wisconsin athletics came from the success of the Wisconsin boxing team, which won its seventh National Collegiate Athletic Association title in 1954.

As the Korean War reached a stalemate and the Eisenhower administration helped bring stability to the country, there was little immediate inclination or momentum for social reform. As a result, the 1950s generally are viewed as a period of tranquility, a perception reinforced by such television shows as "Leave It to Beaver" or "Father Knows Best." Yet an undercurrent of anxiety characterized the times, reflecting a fear of outsiders along with an uncertainty about the appropriate American role in international affairs.

Some interesting points of view on the topic emerged from a symposium featuring contributions from distinguished alumni and published in the February 1952 issue of the *Wisconsin Alumnus.* The symposium asked, "What can American universities and their alumni, *especially their alumni,* do to preserve the American Way of life?" The concern would be sounded again ten years later in a February 1962 symposium when the *Alumnus* asked the same question and observed, "There is no need to remind Americans that we are in a death struggle with the communists."

For the most part, faculty and students remained generally subdued on the issue. Some of the hesitancy was influenced by the personal attacks on governmental officials and others which were leveled by Wisconsin's junior senator, Joseph R. McCarthy. Those who expected students to serve as the conscience of the society were disturbed by a trend toward conformity. Students of the 1950s consequently were characterized as the Silent Generation, even though many strongly questioned Senator McCarthy's motives and tactics.

The regents, reflecting a concern that students needed a proper grounding in American values, adopted a policy requiring undergraduates to take at least one course in American history or government and politics as part of their degree requirements. While the campus remained comparatively calm, change rustled underfoot. Early moves were under way to promote greater student participation in university activities and governance, including student representation on the board of regents.

One of the most influential episodes of the period occurred in 1958, when a group of students brought forward a petition which said that undergraduate education should be more challenging and students should have a greater opportunity to explore topics of special interest. The petitioners included a future congressman, William Steiger, and Gar Alperowitz, who later became a prominent authority on international policy development. The student challenge shook the apparent complacency of the faculty about the level and quality of undergraduate education and provided an impetus for development of the Honors Program in the College of Letters and Science.

Change also came in other ways. Although the enrollment had dropped from a high of 18,693 in 1947–1948 to 13,346 in 1953–1954, there was no question that it would begin to climb again. The new Department of Planning and Construction began to prepare plans for a steady growth of the campus.

Several programs during the 1950s responded to a growing diversity of the student population as well as a change in educational technology. The Integrated Liberal Studies Program (ILS), begun in 1949, provided an updated variation of the Experimental College of the 1920s. It focused on broad liberal studies based on an examination of classical texts studied in a tutorial setting. The new program, as director and professor of English Robert C. Pooley explained, provided "a 'small college' atmosphere on the campus of a great university."

A comparable experiment of the early 1950s was a small-scale program sponsored by the Ford Foundation. High-school-age students received scholarships to enroll in the university before possible induction into the military. Classics professor Herbert M. Howe served as mentor of the program, which saw the precocious young men achieving grade point averages above those of average freshmen in Letters and Science.

Such examples of personalized instruction contrasted with concerns about increasing the "productivity" of education through the use of television. The establishment of a university station helped explore television's educational potential. WHA–TV made its initial broadcasts on May 3, 1954, using makeshift studios located in the old Chemical Engineering Building at 600 North Park Street. The station began a steady, if limited, schedule of programs. The early programs were a mixture of entertainment and education, ranging from the award-winning children's program "The Friendly Giant" to closed-circuit instructional programming.

In addition to reaching out to the state through the media, the university established itself in a number of Wisconsin communities through its two-year centers. Originally the centers had helped absorb some of the enrollment pressure that came after World War II. After the veterans completed their studies, the centers' principal focus shifted to providing freshman and sophomore instruction and serving as "feeder" institutions for the Madison campus.

Changes in the state's budgeting pattern had a marked influence on the scope and pace of growth. Future development was to be based on a regular listing of needs rather than the sporadic appeal for new facilities that had been the previous pattern.

One of the most obvious needs was for additional student housing. In 1953, with enrollment approaching 13,500, only 2,500 university residence hall spaces existed on campus. New construction had to be initiated to provide additional housing, particularly for women and married students. Housing capacity doubled by the end of the decade to accommodate the growing diversity of the student population. The new Chadbourne Hall replaced the original Ladies Hall, which had been a campus fixture since 1871. The Wisconsin Center, another significant campus addition, expanded the university's facilities for continuing and adult education and provided administrative headquarters for the University of Wisconsin Foundation.

The renewed attention given to the university's building program made it obvious that the faculty required continued development and nurture. Higher education expanded across the country during the 1950s. Private colleges and universities grew at a rate similar to public institutions. Increased demand for high-quality faculty produced intense recruitment competition, particularly in agriculture, engineering, and medicine. In 1956 the regents made a special appeal to the legislature for salary adjustments to help retain the faculty. Although the regents did not receive the $478,000 they requested, they were granted $250,000 for distribution on a merit basis to professors and associate professors.

The continuing problem of faculty retention was highlighted in 1958 when Joshua Lederberg received the first Nobel Prize ever granted to a UW faculty member. The recognition came just as Lederberg prepared to leave the University of Wisconsin for Stanford University, where he became head of medical genetics. Nevertheless, the presentation of the award helped to focus attention on the university's considerable contributions to science.

The 1950s produced administrative changes that eventually would have a profound impact on the scope and content of public higher education in Wisconsin. In 1953 Governor Walter Kohler, Jr., proposed the "integration" of all the state's higher educational institutions into a single University of Wisconsin System to be headed by a chancellor. The idea was not new; it had its roots in the late nineteenth century, when an effort was mounted to merge the university and the public normal schools. Similar bills had been introduced in 1909, 1911, 1913, and 1949.

While Kohler lacked the necessary political leverage to achieve integration on his own terms, he had stimulated enough interest in the issue to engineer a compromise. Legislation passed in 1955 merged the Wisconsin State College in Milwaukee and University Extension in Milwaukee into a single institution to be administered by the university. At the same time, the legislature established the Coordinating Committee for Higher Education "to recommend necessary changes in programs and facilities, to provide for a single, consolidated, biennial budget request . . . and to report the results of its studies and recommendations to the governor and the legislature."

The creation of the University of Wisconsin–Milwaukee had important consequences for the University of Wisconsin. It provided an urban university in a time when there was increased interest in and awareness of the special nature and problems of cities, and it enhanced the variety of higher educational opportunities for the citizens of the state.

As the governor and the legislature explored the merits and demerits of integration, a special legislative study also reviewed the scope and status of the University of Wisconsin. Under the auspices of the Wisconsin Legislative Council, the study group included two university alumni who would later serve as governor—Warren Knowles, chairman of the committee, and Gaylord Nelson.

The report anticipated increased enrollments, particularly in graduate studies, which would require reconditioning and remodeling existing buildings and the construction of new facilities. Suggested solutions included expanding the two-year centers and exploring the possibility of interstate cooperation before expansion into other professional fields. The overriding concern, however, was excellence: "Quality rather than quantity, should be the main goal of the University," the report emphasized.

The Regent Committee on the Future Development of the University published a much bolder and more comprehensive report in 1961. This report emerged from a two-year study headed by Regent George E. Watson, state superintendent of public instruction, and came as the nation's interest in higher education experienced a dramatic rise.

The regents' report emphasized "balanced development of the University, with attention to instruction, research and public service." Anticipating a rapidly increasing enrollment, it called for more staff and facilities in Madison and Milwaukee and at the two-year centers. The regents assumed that each of these components would develop a special identity based on its location and the constituency it served. The report also called for improved instruction (particularly at the freshman and sophomore levels), "increasing opportunities for honors and other special work," increased counseling services, the elimination of low-enrollment courses, and increased efforts to reduce the dropout rate.

The regents noted that research should be expanded as an important part of "enriching instruction, and for the service it performs for the people of Wisconsin, the national government and society in general." Public service efforts should follow similar lines but would be increasingly oriented toward urban problems and needs and would respond to continuing education needs generated by "our fast-advancing technology."

In discussing ways to finance this broad and expanding program, the regents called for a doubling of the state appropriation and advocated a "return to the traditional concept of free public higher education." This statement strongly expressed the concept that public higher education existed for the benefit of the total republic and should be accessible to all. "In no case," the regents said, "should fees be allowed to deny education for Wisconsin youngsters of promise, nor should they be used to control enrollments."

The regents recognized federal support and private giving as key elements to finance expansion and provide for items which could not be supported through regular appropriations or student fees. Private gifts and grants, they noted, create "'risk capital' for experimental programs, provide student scholarships and loans, and enable the University to broaden cultural activities and carry on special projects for which state funds are not available."

The regents' document became a blueprint for university actions over the next several years. It also provided the most articulate explanation of the forces and ideas that had shaped the university during the years following World War II. The University of Wisconsin and other universities across the country were no longer institutions with a comparatively narrow focus centered on undergraduate, graduate, and professional education. The new universities were complex, multifaceted institutions that had grown to serve an amazing number of constituencies. Clark Kerr, then president of the University of California, gave this new educational organism its name—the multiversity.

The broadening of the university's influence and involvement came as E. B. Fred announced that he intended to retire in June 1957, his seventieth year. Ever self-effacing, he encouraged the regents to appoint his successor, but they persuaded him to stay on for another year as the search began for a new president.

In 1958 Joshua Lederberg became the first UW faculty member to be awarded the Nobel Prize. Here he meets with reporters following the announcement of his selection to receive the prize.

Rosa Fred, wife of President E. B. Fred, is shown here being knighted as a distinguished patron at the Memorial Union's 1958 Beefeaters Dinner, held to honor Student Union committee members. Student participants in the investiture included, from left: David Meissner, Clarence Lobb, and Doris Feldman.

The return of the World War II veterans brought large enrollments and consequently large classes, as this picture from a lecture of the time illustrates. Although enrollment dropped slightly at the beginning of the 1950s, it began to rise steadily a short time later, and the large lecture class became an educational fixture of campus life.

Nevertheless, the opportunity for smaller classes still existed, as this photo indicates.

This photo, taken at the Preschool Laboratory, shows the contemporary interest in developing the individual.

In November 1952 Wisconsin received its first invitation to play in the Rose Bowl game. When the announcement was made, students skipped classes and flocked to the Memorial Union for a massive celebration and pep rally.

Chemistry professor Farrington Daniels anticipated the future in the 1950s when he conducted experiments on the use of solar energy. This technology became more prominent as a possible energy source in the 1970s, when Middle Eastern oil suppliers instituted an embargo. Daniels is shown here with one of his solar cookers, which used a reflector to capture and focus the sun's rays.

Perhaps the most important educational event on the campus during the 1950s was the opening of the Memorial Library in the fall of 1953.

Here, professor emeritus L. C. Burke brings the first book, a copy of the Coverdale Bible, to be deposited in the new library. Welcoming him are, from left,

President E. B. Fred, regent and former governor Oscar Rennebohm, library director Gilbert Doane, and Letters and Science dean Mark Ingraham.

This photo of a small portion of the card catalog in the new library reflects the growing extensiveness of the university's collections. The increase in the library's holdings also provided a particularly pointed example of the growth in knowledge that accelerated in this period.

Building on the educational leadership it had established through the development of WHA radio and the Statewide Radio Network, the university initiated work in the study of television production and in the broadcast of educational programming. WHA–TV went on the air in 1954 with a regular schedule that included programs ranging from "The Friendly Giant" to those that gave helpful hints on horticulture.

The university intensified and broadened its research activity during the 1950s. Here Professor Charles Edson studies a Macedonian inscription, one of those he subsequently compiled into a volume which provides an important resource for classical studies.

The university, through its Department of Meteorology, was an early leader in climatological studies. Here Reid Bryson (left) and Charles Stearns use newly developed instruments to take measurements on Lake Mendota.

The university continued its tradition of lake studies initiated with the work of Edward A. Birge with the establishment of the Limnology Laboratory under the direction of Arthur Hasler. Here students practice skin-diving techniques while working from one of the university's research vessels, as a photographer makes an appropriate record of the activity.

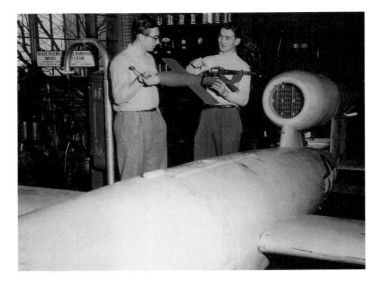

In the early 1950s jet propulsion was still relatively new to engineering faculty and students. A model of a German buzz bomb used against Britain during the waning months of World War II provided students with an example of an application of the new technology.

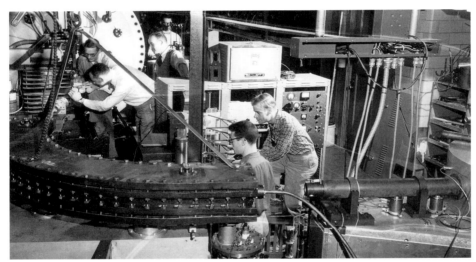

The study of atomic physics experienced dramatic growth following the war. The university, through a consortium called the Midwest Universities Research Association (MURA), built an accelerator on a farm south of Madison and established the Synchrotron Radiation Center and the Physical Sciences Laboratory to provide researchers access to equipment which could generate high-energy particles.

Increased sophistication in technological instruments also led to more precise research and the collateral use of teaching aids such as this enlarged model of the spinal cord being examined by medical students.

Wisconsin's most renowned and often flamboyant architect, Frank Lloyd Wright, received an honorary doctor of fine arts degree in 1955. Wright had been a student at the university in the 1880s and served as an assistant to Allan D. Conover in the construction of Science Hall.

One of the most popular figures on campus for a generation was Carson Gulley, who came to the university in 1926 and served as head chef in the residence halls for twenty-seven years. While a member of the university staff, he trained a number of cooks, bakers, and chefs who went on to careers in food service. He published two books on cooking and, following his retirement, operated a local catering service and conducted a television show on cooking. Carson Gulley Commons in the Lakeshore Halls area is dedicated to his memory.

As the university community grew in size and complexity, it became necessary to establish a police force to protect property and oversee activity on the campus. In the early 1950s the university had six fully deputized officers patrolling the campus and outlying areas. Four are shown here: James Crary, Jerold Reis, Glen Fisher, and Joe Hammersley. Hammersley headed the force and became something of a campus institution due to his oftentimes zealous efforts to uphold moral standards among the students.

Throughout the 1950s the Memorial Union continued to flourish as a focus for university life. Tripp Commons was a popular luncheon rendezvous for faculty, staff, and students.

The completion of the Memorial Library eliminated the need for the Quonset huts on the Lower Campus. This photo, taken in 1953, shows the last of the huts being dismantled and removed.

University enrollment began a steady and dramatic climb beginning in the mid-1950s. This photo shows a freshman convocation held in the Field House. A decade later such events were discontinued, because the size of the incoming freshman class made them unwieldy and difficult to stage.

The tradition of a springtime honors program for senior women continued well into the 1950s. This photo shows the 1950 Senior Swingout, which honored scholarship winners and introduced the new members of Crucible, the junior women's honor society, and Mortar Board, the senior women's honor society.

"Pier-time" has been a historical springtime and summer ritual, as students take advantage of the sunshine and the location of the campus on the shores of Lake Mendota to find an inviting place to study or simply to take time off and cultivate a tan.

The feminist revolution hadn't quite arrived in the 1950s. There were still strong signs of traditional attitudes, as is obvious from this 1950 photo of the judging panel interviewing candidates to be selected as Badger Beauties. Those selected served as the court of honor for the Junior Prom and had their pictures featured in a special section of the Badger *yearbook.*

In the meantime, the annual Haresfoot production still featured men dressed as women.

Nevertheless, winds of change were beginning to blow. Women cheerleaders joined men on the sidelines in 1957 for the first time.

Just before the outbreak of hostilities in Korea, some students expressed their concern over what they perceived to be a continued posture of United States militarism as they picketed the annual spring ROTC review.

The Wisconsin Idea, *a student literary publication published in the early 1950s by the Athenaean Society, provided an outlet for student creativity. The magazine's faculty adviser was Helen C. White, distinguished scholar of English literature and an inspirational teacher. Her memory is perpetuated in the building named after her, which contains the departments of English and philosophy, the School of Library and Information Studies, and the College Library for undergraduates.*

The comic strip Pogo, created by Walt Kelly, was a favorite of college students and faculty during the fifties. Kelly responded to that interest with this special drawing created for the *1951* Badger.

A traditionally popular aspect of Homecoming at Camp Randall is the lawyers' cane toss, initiated in *1910*. Senior law students parade onto the field before the game carrying canes. After a ceremonial march down the field, they toss their canes over the crossbar of the goalpost. If they catch the canes they supposedly will win their first cases.

The 1949 Badger cross country team demonstrated athletic togetherness as they joined hands in crossing the finish line during the Marquette meet held on the agricultural campus. The Badgers took their second consecutive Big Ten title that season and finished seventh in the NCAA meet.

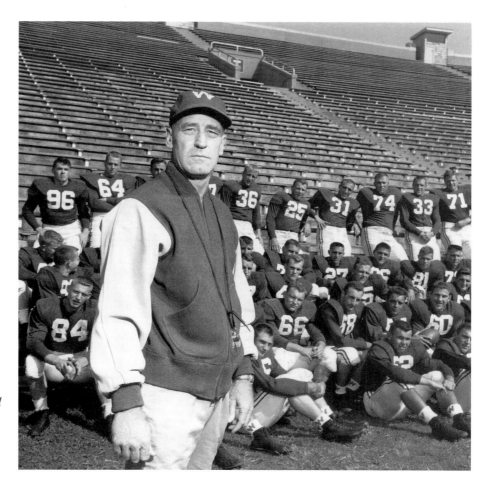

Ivan Williamson was Wisconsin's most successful football coach of the modern era. Williamson coached from 1949 to 1955 and established a record of 41–19–4, including a Big Ten championship and Wisconsin's first trip to the Rose Bowl in 1953.

Boxing continued to be a popular winter sports attraction, as the Badgers remained a national power throughout the decade. Here light heavyweight Ray Zale squares off against a Penn State opponent.

The job interview became a part of the undergraduate ritual for many students during the 1950s. The university established the Career Advising and Placement Service in the late 1940s, and students regularly consulted bulletin boards for prospects of life beyond graduation.

Growth,
Change,
and
Turmoil

The selection of Conrad A. Elvehjem as E. B. Fred's successor represented a vote for continuity. Born in McFarland, Elvehjem was, like Van Hise, a Wisconsin native and university alumnus. He had a distinguished career as a biochemist, gaining particular recognition for his discovery that nicotinic acid (niacin) could be used to treat pellagra. His wife, the former Constance Waltz, also graduated from the University of Wisconsin and became the first alumna to assume the responsibilities of a president's wife.

Although he may have seemed to represent a continuation of what had gone before, Elvehjem came to the presidency in 1958 as the nation and higher education were experiencing substantial change. Chemistry professor Farrington Daniels noted that Elvehjem faced "up to what he called the twin challenges of rising enrollments in the universities and expanding knowledge." This expanding knowledge led to a more complex society, one heavily reliant on technology for its progress and cohesiveness. More college-trained people were needed to sustain and expand the progress that accompanied the technological development. This need had an obvious impact on the university. The student population had dropped from its previous all-time high of 18,623 in 1947–1948 to 13,346 in 1953–1954, but then began a steady rise. As Elvehjem assumed the presidency in 1958–1959, enrollment had reversed its previous drop and climbed to 17,145.

Research, often primed by outside funding, showed a parallel expansion. One clear example was the endowment provided through the estate of William McArdle to underwrite a comprehensive program of cancer research. McArdle Laboratory illustrated the increased complexity and interrelatedness of research and scholarly inquiry on the campus. Other examples of increased cooperative research came from the Institute for Research in the Humanities, the Army Mathematics Research Center, the Institute for Research on Poverty, the Center for the Study of Public Policy and Administration (which later became the La Follette Institute for Public Affairs), the Theoretical Chemistry Institute, and the *Dictionary of American Regional English* (*DARE*).

The Enzyme Institute pointed to the growing specialization of knowledge. Established in 1948 through a grant from the Wisconsin Alumni Research Foundation, the institute housed research teams formed to investigate specific aspects of the chemistry of life.

A continuing expansion and even urgency described university activity on a number of fronts at the beginning of the 1960s. Elvehjem moved the university deliberately forward, meeting with controversy on occasion. The most prominent episode involved John Z. Bowers, dean of the Medical School, who provoked a divisive dispute when he proposed the appointment of an outside person as head of the surgery department. After a considerable review of the situation, and on recommendation of the president, the regents fired Bowers in October 1961.

The wounds inflicted through this incident had not healed when Conrad Elvehjem died unexpectedly in July 1962. The regents moved quickly to fill the administrative void. After consulting with key faculty and administrative representatives, they chose Fred Harvey Harrington, an expert on American diplomatic history who had been an unsuccessful candidate for the UW presidency when E. B. Fred had retired four years earlier. Harrington, a faculty member for twenty-five years, had been appointed vice president for academic affairs when Elvehjem became president.

Although selected to replace Elvehjem, Harrington had accepted an offer to become president of the University of Hawaii just before Elvehjem died. Eager to preserve a continuity of leadership, the regents quickly persuaded him to accept the Wisconsin presidency and secured his release from the Hawaii commitment.

Harrington's inauguration in October 1962 came at the time of the Morrill Act centennial. The new president recognized that the time was ripe for innovative expansion. Broad change, however, required a new administrative structure. The president established the central administration to oversee and coordinate development at the various UW campuses and related units. The board of regents continued setting policy on fiscal and administrative matters.

In January 1965 the regents approved title changes for three top administrators: Robben W. Fleming, Madison; J. Martin Klotsche, Milwaukee; and Lorenz H. Adolfson, University Centers. Their prior designation of provost was changed to chancellor, reflecting similar usage in complex universities such as California, North Carolina, and Missouri. A short time later, Harrington restructured extension activity by combining agricultural and cooperative extension with general extension and by consolidating related support services into a single administrative unit with its own chancellor.

New developments and issues which accompanied a shift in the pattern of funding for the university's operation became an obvious concern. The percentages which state appropriations and tuition and fees contributed to the total operating budget had shrunk proportionately as the size of the university increased. Funding for expansion of research and for increased programming came from grants, primarily from the federal government and foundations, and from a rise in private giving.

As other developments proceeded, the faculty sought ways to maintain its primary responsibility for the development of academic policy and programs. This required coordination of activity across the entire university at the same time that each campus maintained policies fitted to its distinctive needs. The University Faculty Council was created in 1966, and the University Faculty Assembly in 1967.

While administrative and policy developments went forward, new buildings provided graphic evidence of change. The period from 1959 to 1971 saw an incredible surge of construction at Madison. The boom became a race to accommodate the steadily increasing enrollments and to provide the space needed for the expansion of research. Federal and state money primarily funded the construction, but bond issues financed projects like housing, while private gifts supported other projects, such as the Nielsen Tennis Stadium and the Elvehjem Museum of Art.

The immediate impact of increased enrollments came in the building of new dormitory space, which more than doubled in ten years. The initial signal of the change was the new Chadbourne Hall dormitory. Concurrent with its construction was the addition of new dormitories for men and women in the Elm Drive area at the western end of the campus. The most intense concentration and massive development came during the period 1961–1965 with the creation of the Southeast Dormitory area, a high-rise complex which added two thousand spaces for men and women in two blocks just east of Park Street between Johnson and Dayton streets. The construction of the David Schreiner and Zoe Bayliss houses initiated a university-sponsored experiment in cooperative living. A contingent of married students occupied the first units of Eagle Heights apartments constructed in the wooded area north of University Bay Marsh.

The key document for the development of the campus during this period was the Sketch Plan adopted in 1959. It became the most comprehensive outline of proposed and recommended campus development since the Cret, Laird, and Peabody plan of 1908. The plan reaffirmed the principles established nearly half a century earlier "to utilize the natural beauty of the site," to develop portions of the campus along functional lines, and to provide for expansion as well as sufficient space to minimize high-density concentrations. The plan also contained two new items not considered in the 1908 plan: parking and the conflict between pedestrian and vehicular traffic.

The Sketch Plan assumed that enrollment would nearly double in slightly more than ten years, rising from 16,590 in the fall of 1958 to 30,000 in 1970. This called for expansion south of University Avenue, a major departure from previous plans and agreements about campus boundaries. Some saw the proposed expansion as the beginning of a drive to engulf a significant portion of the central city. This concern led to the establishment of a City-University Coordinating Committee to increase communication and to monitor additional developments that would affect the neighborhoods adjoining the campus.

While the principal emphasis was on the construction of new research facilities and on classroom buildings, three major libraries also were built during this period: the Steenbock Library on the agricultural campus, the Middleton Medical Library, and the College Library for undergraduates. A new Extension Building on Lake Street consolidated many of the various extension functions combined through the merger. Intercollegiate athletics benefited from the construction of a new Crew House. The addition of an upper deck to the west side of Camp Randall Stadium provided a new communications center and twelve thousand seats, bringing the total stadium capacity to more than seventy-eight thousand.

By the mid-1960s, with enrollment rapidly approaching thirty thousand students, the potential for university growth seemed almost limitless. In a 1965 interview with the *Daily Cardinal*, Harrington noted, "In the last six years there has been more building in Madison than in the whole previous history of the campus. The building program has amounted to a million dollars worth a week for the past two years, mostly in Madison."

Two new four-year campuses, at Green Bay and in the Racine-Kenosha area (UW–Parkside), added to the university's statewide profile. Not just additional colleges added as a means of accommodating surplus enrollment, these new institutions responded to new ideas about the scope and content of postsecondary education. The curricula at Green Bay and Parkside were to be eclectic, centering on the rapidly changing nature of contemporary life. Green Bay would focus on the environment and communication.

Parkside, because of its location in one of Wisconsin's industrial communities, would concentrate on industry and technology.

The locations of the new institutions combined with those of existing UW campuses created a triangle that stretched from Green Bay to Madison to Milwaukee and Racine-Kenosha. The major portion of the state's citizens resided within or near the triangle. The potential political impact of that distribution significantly influenced competition for educational resources between the university and the state colleges. This competition was highlighted when the state colleges petitioned for a change in their status. Their leadership argued that the scope of their educational activity had far outdistanced their original mission of teacher training. The competition for resources helped underscore the arguments of those advocating combining all the state's institutions of higher education into a single system.

The university, meanwhile, received important infusions of outside support. In 1960 proceeds from the estate of Colonel William F. Vilas became available. Vilas, a Civil War hero, lumberman, public servant, and university regent, had died in 1908, leaving a trust to be used for various university projects. Income from the trust provided undergraduate scholarships and graduate fellowships. It also created the Vilas research professorships, which freed certain distinguished university faculty from a full load of teaching and administrative responsibilities so they could concentrate on research.

In addition to this important windfall, the growth of the University of Wisconsin Foundation produced additional income. Celebrating its fifteenth anniversary in 1960, the foundation noted its extensive and varied contributions to university life. The most important item was the Wisconsin Center, a facility for continuing education, located at the corner of Lake and Langdon streets. Further contributions by the foundation included professorships, fellowships, and scholarships.

The development of University Hill Farms on the western edge of Madison provided another important source of income. Six hundred acres of farmland were transformed into a neighborhood of single-family homes and multifamily units anchored by a large shopping center called Hilldale. The sale of lots and the operation of the shopping center (opened in 1962) provided capital to purchase the Arlington Farms in the northeastern corner of Dane County. This site offered approximately twelve hundred acres for an experimental farm and research center for the College of Agriculture. Hilldale income also provided an endowment to support a number of projects, including professorships and a lecture series.

In addition to the growing contributions of the University of Wisconsin Foundation, the Wisconsin Alumni Research Foundation quietly but steadily expanded its support of university research. Private giving also became increasingly important. Mr. and Mrs. A. C. Nielsen, for example, gave more than a million dollars in 1966 to underwrite the construction of an indoor tennis facility on the western edge of the campus.

The expansion which characterized other areas of the university during the 1960s also influenced the development of the academic program. Technology produced new machines for learning which could be used as creative adjuncts to the traditional methods of classroom instruction. Technology also advanced and expanded off-campus instruction. The Educational Telephone Network (ETN) and the Statewide Extension Education Network (SEEN) connected the campus with each county courthouse and other specialized sites. This made it possible to conduct conferences, seminars, and staff development or in-service training programs for those who could not afford the cost or take the time to travel to a conventional classroom location. The network also accommodated administrative teleconferences, reducing the need for expensive and time-consuming travel to a central location.

Interinstitutional cooperation became increasingly common. The Midwest Universities Research Association (MURA), a consortium of fourteen universities initiated at Madison, promoted the development of research in high-energy physics. This led to the development of the Synchrotron Radiation Center and the Physical Sciences Laboratory near Stoughton. The Biotron, located on the western edge of the campus, provided a highly sophisticated research machine capable of duplicating any climatic environment found on earth. Experimentation took on an extraterrestrial dimension as astronomy professor Arthur D. Code and his colleagues developed instrumentation for Orbital Astronomical Observatories (OAO) designed to make observations from satellites positioned outside the earth's atmosphere.

Dramatic advancements in both technology and knowledge created new fields of scholarship and research. University departments and academic specialties expanded into such areas as nuclear engineering, nuclear physics, molecular biology, food microbiology and toxicology, computer engineering, computer sciences, women's studies, and Afro-American studies.

The broadening of research reflected growth elsewhere. The number of University of Wisconsin Centers expanded in response to enrollment pressures and the desire of local communities to benefit from the educational and cultural resources offered by institutions of higher education. Construction costs for the local facilities were funded by the county, while the university provided staffing to operate the program. Under this arrangement, new centers were established during the early 1960s in the Fox Valley (Menasha), Green

Bay, Kenosha, Manitowoc, Marathon County (Wausau), Marshfield (Wood County), and Sheboygan County. A short time later, additional centers were built in Waukesha County, Rock County, West Bend (Washington County), and Baraboo (Sauk County).

First and most obvious, the centers offered students an economical means of gaining access to higher education close to home. For many, they also provided an important testing ground: students could determine whether they were sufficiently qualified for college work or interested in transferring to a degree-granting institution. Those who completed their first two years of study earned an associate degree. The centers also offered opportunities in continuing education for nontraditional students and served as a focus for cultural and intellectual activity in the community.

As the university nurtured these local opportunities, it also advanced a global perspective for its programs. Harrington had encouraged this development even before he became president. In 1960 he noted that "Wisconsin professors have been on important assignments in Labrador and the Antarctic; in Latin America, Africa and the Middle East; in Australia, Scandinavia and Germany, Yugoslavia and the Soviet Union."

This activity paralleled a growth of United States involvement and commitment around the world and gave the university a new and substantial international dimension. It led to the creation of the Office of International Studies and Programs headed by a dean at the university in Madison. A similar program emerged at the University of Wisconsin–Milwaukee. The international perspective was incorporated into the curriculum and research through programs in Southeast Asian, African, Ibero-American, and Luso-Brazilian studies. These were augmented by Junior Year Abroad programs.

Not only were faculty involved in programs that took them to all corners of the world, but the campus at Madison continued to maintain its traditional position as host to one of the largest contingents of foreign students in the country. The resultant polyglot community charged the campus with an atmosphere of startling cultural diversity. Further impetus for international education and development came in 1964 through MUCIA, the Midwest Universities Corsortium for International Activities, Inc. The Ford Foundation provided the means to establish MUCIA as a private consortium of eight land-grant, Big Ten universities: Illinois, Indiana, Iowa, Michigan State, Minnesota, Ohio State, Purdue, and Wisconsin.

The growing egalitarian makeup of the student population along with the steadily climbing enrollment created a new dynamic at Madison and at other colleges and universities around the country. A strength in numbers gave the 1960s student generation a sense of self-awareness that had not existed before. As more students went on to college, the enrollment included a broader representation from all levels of society. The campus became a stage for acting out tensions present in the larger society. The resulting activity produced the most turbulent decade in the university's history.

The 1960s tumult began on a rather traditional note of collegiate high jinks. A destructive outburst of enthusiasm on the Lower Campus and State Street followed a 1962 Badger football victory over Notre Dame. While it produced property damage, the incident merely hinted at coming events. By the mid-1960s the focus of student activity began to change considerably. Concerns about enlargement of the war in Vietnam and involvement in the civil rights movement shaped a considerable portion of student activity.

During 1964–1965, a series of free speech demonstrations at the University of California at Berkeley captured the headlines and a major spot on the evening television news. This had a galvanizing effect on students across the country, introducing an era of massive student demonstrations. A teach-in dealing with the war in Vietnam was held on the Madison campus in the spring of 1965. During the same period students launched a vigorous protest against representatives of the United States State Department who came to explain the government's policy in Southeast Asia. A series of antidraft protests, including an extended sit-in at the administration building, rocked the campus the following spring. In February 1967 students demonstrated against the presence of recruiters from Dow Chemical Company. Dow, they said, was guilty of war crimes because it manufactured the napalm used in Vietnam. Seventeen students were arrested. Chancellor Robben Fleming used a personal check for $1,155 to bail eleven of the students out of jail, explaining that he did not want to deal with the substance of the issue while students were still in jail. Many saw his move and its rationale as a sign of weakness and conciliation at a time that called for firmness.

The incident occurred as the momentum of protest tilted toward the issue of student self-determination. The watchword of the moment became "Student power," as the Wisconsin Student Association adopted a bill in April 1967 proclaiming that students "should govern themselves and regulate their lives and interests democratically through WSA."

On October 18, 1967, students again demonstrated against Dow Chemical, blocking hallways in the Commerce Building, the site of the job interviews. Police summoned reinforcements as the situation deteriorated into a disruptive confrontation that produced property damage and injuries to both police and demonstrators.

Intense protest activity again seized the campus late in the winter of 1969. A group of students presented a list of thirteen "non-negotiable" demands to the administration in a move to secure greater representation and rights for black students and faculty. This precipitated a student "strike" which lasted for most of February.

Initially, university officers, supplemented by city and state police reinforcements, managed the protests. After a few days of intensive involvement, however, they found their resources stretched thin. Chancellor Edwin Young appealed to Governor Warren Knowles to activate a contingent of the National Guard as relief for the regular police forces. During the course of the strike, forty-five people (including thirty-six students) were arrested on various charges. The eventual by-products of the strike included the establishment of the Afro-American Studies department and the creation of a special five-year program to provide counseling, guidance, and scholarship opportunities for minority students.

As the war in Southeast Asia churned on with no foreseeable resolution, feelings of unease and discontent grew at home. The year 1970 proved pivotal. Early in February a mysterious fire caused damage to the Army ROTC headquarters housed in a portion of the Old Red Gym. A short time later, a demonstration against recruiters from General Electric, a major defense contractor, deteriorated into a destructive foray.

In March teaching assistants went out on strike for twenty-five days in a dispute over such issues as class size, length of appointment, and evaluation. The campus had hardly settled down from this major interruption of the academic routine when United States troops, responding to orders from President Richard Nixon, launched an incursion into Cambodia, further escalating the war in Southeast Asia. Another national incident followed almost immediately. Ohio National Guard troops fired into a crowd of antiwar protesters on the campus of Kent State University and killed four young people. Two tumultuous weeks of protest closed out the semester on the Madison campus. As before, outside police forces and National Guard troops were summoned to help maintain order, and the faculty and administration struggled to find a satisfactory means to conclude the semester following the weeks of recurrent disruption.

The summer brought a momentary lull, but no peace. On August 24, 1970, a home-made bomb placed in a van parked in the alley just off Charter Street between Sterling Hall and the Old Chemistry Building exploded and shattered the sleepy morning calm of late summer. The explosion, directed at the Army Math Research Center housed in Sterling Hall, caused more than two million dollars worth of property damage and took the life of Robert Fassnacht, a graduate student in physics who was in the building.

The Sterling Hall bombing served as a watershed. Protest activity continued, but not at the extreme level that had characterized demonstrations in the late 1960s and 1970. A loss of public confidence and the introduction of entitlement programs which came with President Lyndon Johnson's Great Society initiatives had eroded the national and state resolve to support higher education. New social priorities and programs placed a claim on available public funds. The resources which had been so extensively and willingly supplied throughout the 1960s would not be as readily forthcoming in the future.

The university's thirteenth president, Conrad A. Elvehjem, was born in McFarland, grew up in the shadow of the university, and spent his entire career at the university as a student, faculty member, and administrator. This portrait by Aaron Bohrod depicts elements from Elvehjem's background along with highlights of his scientific career.

Fred Harvey Harrington became the university's fourteenth president following Elvehjem's untimely death. A historian, Harrington assumed leadership at a time when the university experienced its most substantial period of growth.

The 1960s began with a sense of optimism. Senator John F. Kennedy was one of the vanguard promising to bring new energy and perspectives to government and public life. He is shown here speaking at the UW Field House in October 1960 as he campaigned successfully for president of the United States.

While ROTC still played a significant role in providing officer candidates for the armed forces, it also reflected shifts in the makeup of the military. This photo shows newly commissioned navy officers welcoming Gay W. Rost to their midst. A Nursing School graduate, she was the first woman commissioned into the navy from the university.

Although change rustled in the air, a number of traditional student activities still were very much in evidence, such as this County Fair sponsored by the Memorial Union.

The burden of studying did not get any easier in the 1960s. Students were often overwhelmed by the number of textbooks they had to purchase for a given semester, as this photo, taken at the University Book Store, shows.

In August 1965 fire destroyed the Journalism Building opposite Science Hall on Observatory Drive. The building was subsequently replaced by Helen C. White Hall.

One of the popular indoor sports of the time was painting graffiti on the walls of the Varsity Bar, a student watering spot on lower State Street.

The assassination of President John F. Kennedy significantly dampened the sense of promise and enthusiasm that began the 1960s. The university community turned out in substantial numbers to participate in a memorial service for the slain president.

Wisconsin native and UW sports legend Elroy Hirsch returned to the university in 1969, when he was named athletic director. His personal magnetism generated a rebirth of enthusiasm for Badger athletics. The program expanded dramatically during his eighteen years of service. He is shown here in the early 1970s boosting Bucky Badger as UW alumnus and Madison banker Robert W. Pohle looks on.

Robben Fleming was named chancellor of the Madison campus in 1965. He was responsible for the day-to-day administration of the university at Madison, while President Fred Harvey Harrington had overall responsibility for the statewide university, which included campuses at Madison, Milwaukee, Green Bay, and Parkside (Racine-Kenosha), the Center System, and Extension.

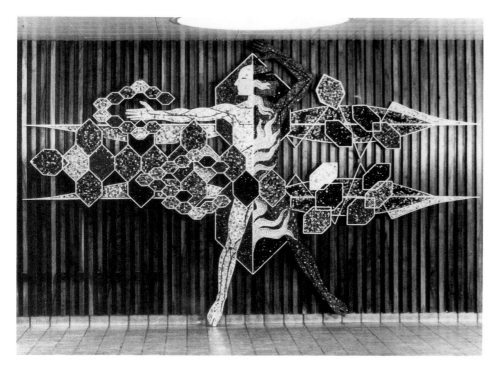

This mosaic by James S. Watrous, UW artist and art historian, was installed in the new Social Studies Building constructed north of the Carillon Tower. Watrous also provided the mural decorations for the Paul Bunyan Room in the Memorial Union as well as mosaics for the Commerce Building, Vilas Communication Hall, and the Memorial Library.

BOOKS ARE THE SEED
WHICH IS RETURNED TO THE SOIL
AS THE CONDITION OF
FURTHER INCREASE
JOHN BASCOM

One thing that remains constant from one generation to the next is that students will *find distinctive ways to relax and take a break from studying. This student outside the* *Memorial Library is either totally relaxed or totally absorbed in his studies.*

As the decade progressed, the 1960s grew into a volatile period of protest and disruption. The era began on a somewhat reactionary note as some students voiced opposition to Fidel Castro's takeover of Cuba. But opposition to the growing United States involvement in Southeast Asia, specifically the sending of increased numbers of troops to Vietnam, soon replaced this sentiment. The rise of protest began with an antidraft demonstration at the Field House and a subsequent sit-in at the administration building. A dramatic confrontation between protesters and police occurred at an anti–Dow Chemical protest in October 1967 at the Commerce Building. Antiwar sentiment surfaced again at the 1968 Spring Commencement. In the late fall of that year a display of crosses on Bascom Hill symbolized the loss of

Americans in the war. A student strike calling for the recruitment of more black students and the presence of more black faculty and staff punctuated the antiwar activity. The extensiveness and size of the strike eventually led to the calling of the National Guard to campus to help keep the university open. The protest movement reached its apex in the spring and summer of 1970: teaching assistants went on strike, and then students held a protracted demonstration in reaction to the United States' incursion into Cambodia and the killing of four students during an antiwar protest at Kent State University. Once again the National Guard was called to the campus to help maintain order. In late summer a bomb exploded outside Sterling Hall, killing a researcher and producing more than two million dollars worth of property damage.

Growth, Change, and Turmoil

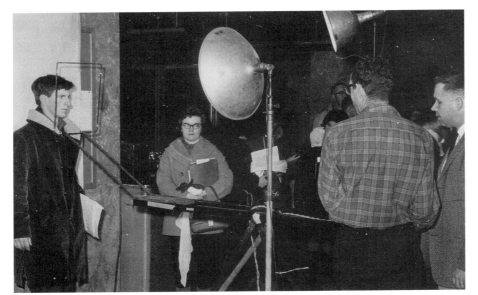

One of the by-products of the frequent campus disruptions was the institution of required photo identification for all students and staff. The equipment used to introduce the process became a routine part of registration.

The turmoil of the late 1960s stimulated university efforts to actively seek minority students at all levels. This photo, taken in the Law Library, particularly symbolizes the effort. The mural in the background is John Steuart Curry's Freeing of the Slaves.

Graffiti blossomed throughout the campus during the 1960s. The plywood fences that surrounded campus construction sites provided convenient surfaces for expression. They became bulletin boards for the expression of everything from political activism to philosophical angst. They also provided the time-honored opportunity for promotion. Here artist-in-residence Aaron Bohrod decorates the construction fence around the Humanities Building to call attention to WHA–TV.

Technology continued to provide new opportunities for research and instruction. Students in Professor Laurens Anderson's general biochemistry class created this forest of molecules as part of an exercise familiarizing them with the complex structures of proteins.

The work of Professor Verner E. Suomi (left) pioneered new research horizons. A member of the meteorology department and founder of the Space Science and Engineering Center, Suomi led the Wisconsin team which developed a number of instrumentation satellites used to measure radiation and the heat balance of the earth. He won the National Medal of Science in 1977.

Suomi's experiments required sophisticated instrumentation. Here scientist Harry Miller looks through an instrument designed to collect and store radiation data gathered from outer space.

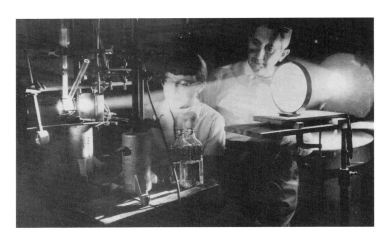

Botany professor John Stauffer (right) uses an ultraviolet light beam as part of his research activity. Stauffer developed a strain of penicillin which led to a doubling of the world's production without increasing the number or size of the manufacturing plants.

This huge two-hundred-ton press tested the strength and properties of cement and concrete as part of the university's research in civil engineering.

Although technology provided new techniques and instrumentation for instruction, some of the time-honored resources continued to be utilized effectively. Here the university's pioneering dance instructor, Margaret H'Doubler, who began her work in the 1920s, uses a skeleton to demonstrate aspects of movement and their relation to dance.

History professor Michael Petrovich, a campus pioneer in using a multimedia approach to instruction, here conducts a class in a special instructional laboratory set up in the Education Building. Petrovich's courses in Russian history were noted for their richness of information and his use of images to give an additional dimension to the text and his lectures.

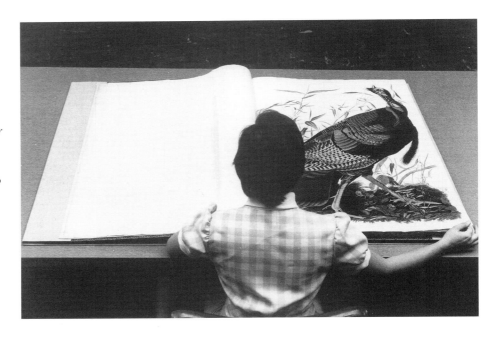

A distinctive strength of the university's General Library System is its rare book and special collections. The 1948 purchase of the collection of history of science books owned by Chester Thordarson initially stimulated growth in this area. Among the collection is a two-volume set of the elephant folio edition of John James Audubon's The Birds of America.

Another important collection is that donated by Mary Renne-bohm (pictured here), featuring works by Wisconsin authors.

Throughout the 1960s the university expanded its language instruction and became one of the nation's leaders in the diversity of its offerings. The program included courses ranging from classical Greek and Latin to Hindi and Telegu. Here, Kuo-Ping Chou offers instruction in Chinese ideograms.

Tapes effectively supplemented instruction. The College of Letters and Science established a specially equipped language laboratory to assist students in pronunciation and comprehension drills.

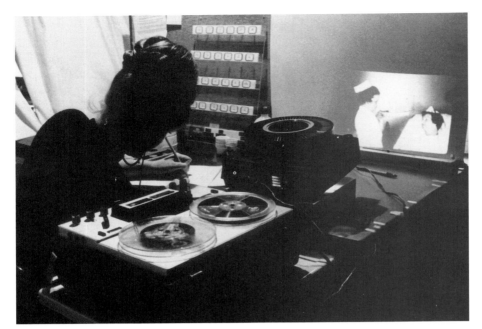

Audiovisual tutorials, such as this one in nursing, also promoted individualized instruction. Subsequently, videotapes helped to reinforce classroom instruction.

Before the advent of the personalized computer and the floppy disk, punch cards assisted in the computerized manipulation of data.

Psychologist Harry F. Harlow led research into various aspects of human behavior as director of the University of Wisconsin Primate Laboratory and the Wisconsin Regional Primate Center. Harlow—shown here with his wife, Margaret, also a behaviorist—conducted experiments that produced a greater understanding of the importance of parental love in promoting social adjustment among the young.

The university continued its strong tradition of research in the life sciences during the 1960s. International recognition of the depth and quality of that research came in 1968, when Har Gobind Khorana, codirector of the Enzyme Institute, won the Nobel Prize for physiology and medicine for his work in developing an understanding of the genetic code.

New perspectives were an important aspect of the university as it grew dramatically in the 1960s. As this view from the top of Van Hise Hall suggests, Bascom Hill was no longer the geographic or administrative center of the university. President Fred Harvey Harrington had moved his office to Van Hise Hall and had developed a central administration which encompassed four-year and two-year campuses around the state. Further expansion occurred in 1971, with the merger of the University of Wisconsin and the Wisconsin state universities.

The Brittingham Fund, a trust established through a bequest from Thomas E. Brittingham, Sr., has continually provided support for projects at the university. During the 1950s and into the 1960s, the trust supported scholarships for Scandinavian students who came to spend a year on the campus. The proponent of the program was Thomas E. Brittingham, Jr., who died in 1960. Here, sixty Viking program alumni return to the campus in 1963 to dedicate a rune stone placed in his honor on Muir Knoll.

Wisconsin did not frequently visit the Rose Bowl, but the 1963 game with Southern California proved to be one of the most exciting in the history of the classic, as the Badgers staged a fourth-quarter rally to score 28 points, only to come up on the short end of a 42–37 score.

One of the most dramatic aspects of university development during the 1960s was the tremendous increase in building. This scene shows the construction of Helen C. White Hall at the intersection of North Park Street and Observatory Drive. The new building, which houses the departments of English and philosophy, the School of Library and Information Studies, and the College Library for undergraduates, was constructed on a site formerly occupied by the Chemical Engineering Building (600 North Park) and the Journalism Building.

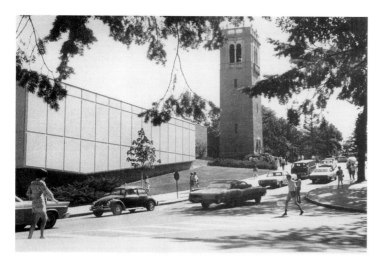

Other notable additions to the campus during the period included the Social Sciences Building, which houses the departments of economics and sociology.

Van Vleck Hall, constructed just south of Bascom Hall between Birge and Sterling halls, presented a particular architectural challenge. It required creating a large volume of space on a relatively small area to accommodate the Department of Mathematics and provide badly needed classroom space in the central campus area.

Not all construction during the 1960s was permanent. This temporary overpass, located between Science Hall and the Memorial Union, became an experiment in reducing the conflict between pedestrian and vehicular traffic on North Park Street at the Langdon Street intersection. As the photo shows, most pedestrians chose to take their chances crossing the street at grade level. Later, a permanent overpass constructed a short distance to the south gained more extensive use as it provided a convenient and unimpeded link between the Humanities Building and the foot of Bascom Hill.

The university assumed a decidedly international flavor during the 1960s. The percentage of international students studying on the campus was one of the highest in the country. Many foreign visitors came to the campus to participate in workshops and training programs. This photo shows a delegation of Congolese officials who came to Madison to study aspects of Wisconsin's state and local government.

The University Band enjoyed rising popularity through the leadership of Professor Raymond F. Dvorak, who served as the director from 1934 to 1968. Here he leads the band in a popular summer concert on the Union Terrace.

Epilogue | A Statewide System for Higher Education

The 1970s ushered in an era that significantly changed the relationship between the university and the state. One could no longer think of the University of Wisconsin at Madison in traditional terms, as the state's primary focus of higher education.

The transition began in 1970. Although the pressure against Fred Harvey Harrington's administration had been building for at least two years, his resignation, announced at the May 8 meeting of the board of regents, caught most people by surprise. Some speculated that had Harrington not resigned, the regents would have fired him. These thoughts were fueled by perceptions that the university administration was unable to control the rising frequency and intensity of student demonstrations and unwilling to summarily separate dissidents from the campus. In an interview with the *Wisconsin State Journal*, Harrington suggested that some had "used student unrest as an excuse rather than the reason for [budget] cuts." He also thought that "if you compare our handling of trouble with other universities, I think you'll feel we have done pretty well. . . . we have managed to get out of some very difficult situations with minimal damage."

Robert L. Clodius, who had served as vice president under Harrington, was appointed acting president as the regents began their search for a replacement who would work more closely with them to quell campus disruptions and consolidate the statewide development of the university. The search led to UW alumnus John C. Weaver, president of the University of Missouri. (The university's first head, John Lathrop, held the same position when called to Madison 121 years earlier.) As the son of speech and theater professor Andrew T. Weaver, John Weaver had grown up on the campus, attending both Wisconsin High School and later the university, where he earned three degrees, including the Ph.D. in geography.

Less than a year after he returned to Madison, Weaver found himself confronted with running an institution substantially different from the one he had known as a student. Legislation passed in October 1971 created the University of Wisconsin System, a federation of institutions that included two-year centers; the state universities, which primarily focused on teaching; doctoral universities at Madison and Milwaukee; and a substantial outreach component through University Extension.

Meanwhile, the university at Madison passed an important benchmark—its one hundred twenty-fifth anniversary. The 1974–1975 observation of the occasion featured a variety of programs, publications, and alumni activities and coincided with the fiftieth anniversary of the Wisconsin Alumni Research Foundation.

The observance formed a backdrop for implementation of the newly signed merger bill. The most immediate indication of the merger was the expansion and consolidation of the board of regents to incorporate regents from the University of Wisconsin and the state universities. The initial concerns of the board centered on process and procedure. The regents had to consider not only the needs of local institutions in the system but also the larger issues that shaped public higher education in the state.

The initial activity of the restructured board of regents was often tedious, painful, and political. As is generally the case, old loyalties died hard. The perspectives and allegiances of the former institutions were embedded in the minds of many of those guiding implementation of the merger. The concept of merger, integrating most of the state's institutions of public higher education, had been a compelling idea in theory. Making it work from a practical standpoint became an extraordinarily complex matter. It involved preserving the identities of the various institutions within the newly formed system while integrating their components, including consolidating the budget and the building program.

Obviously, the first years of merger were transitional, as adjustments were made to new alignments, to new ways of doing things. Weaver, with the assistance of Donald K. Smith, who supervised academic developments, and Donald E. Percy, who coordinated the budget and related matters, steered a careful course through the often choppy political and administrative waters. At the same time, Chancellor Edwin Young found ways to keep what had been identified as the flagship campus—the University of Wisconsin–Madison—from foundering in the rolling seas of change.

The university continued to grow at Madison, stimulated by steady increases in enrollment along with infusions of outside funds that supported faculty research. At the same time, the curriculum had remained relatively stable as reforms had swept across the country at other colleges and universities during the 1960s. The Wisconsin faculty resisted the faddish oscillations in academic programs and generally deflected efforts to offer more "relevant" courses centered on topical issues. New programs were added only when their design and content were consistent with an accepted academic rationale.

Merger routinized change, as academic planning protocols were established to review majors, degree programs, and curriculum changes. New programs or changes in existing programs had to be approved at three levels—the campus, the UW System administration, and the regents.

While these requirements channeled faculty initiative, they did not suppress it. The same energy and inquisitiveness that attracted outside funds to the campus also produced new fields of study and the further subdivision of existing fields of knowledge. Although national concern grew about overspecialization, the Wisconsin tradition of interdisciplinary activity ensured cross-fertilization rather than scholarly isolation.

Faculty quality continued to rank high in the broadest sense. A study of graduate education by the American Council on Education published in 1971 rated universities in thirty-six academic departments. The nationwide poll of six thousand scholars showed the University of Wisconsin–Madison to be strong in thirty departments and good or adequate in six, an evaluation which placed the university solidly among the nation's top ten. In addition, the University of Wisconsin–Madison ranked consistently in the top five in research funding throughout the decade.

The most noteworthy faculty recognition was the 1975 Nobel Prize awarded to cancer researcher Howard Temin for his studies on cancer-causing viruses. Three other Wisconsin scientists received the nation's highest scientific honor, the National Medal of Science: Joseph O. Hirschfelder for his work in theoretical chemistry, Verner E. Suomi for meteorology and space science and engineering, and Robert R. Burris, bacteriologist, for his work on nitrogen fixation.

The intensity and scope of the university's research program significantly influenced the community, attracting and stimulating the development of a number of technology-related businesses in the area. Research, combined with the instructional program and related activities, had a substantial impact on the local and state economy. A 1978 study conducted by Professor William Strang of the University of Wisconsin–Madison Center for Business Development found that the university had contributed more than eight hundred million dollars to the local economy the previous year.

Academic practices that had existed at the university for several decades deepened: consortia, institutes, or centers were established to focus on topics that covered broad areas. In 1970 the university established the Institute for Environmental Studies, primarily in response to growing concerns over the deterioration of the natural environment. The university also became one of five national Sea Grant Institutes. This federally funded program provided researchers in various fields opportunities to study the physical and environmental aspects of the Great Lakes.

The previous decade's momentum in construction carried forward into the 1970s. The most extensive transformation took place on the far western edge of the campus in an area that had once been an experimental muck farm for the College of Agriculture. The area became the site of the Clinical Science Center (CSC), a massive crystal-shaped structure, the largest single complex ever built with state funds. Its projected cost of $88 million eventually grew to an actual cost of $120 million.

The complex contained facilities for patient care, clinical and basic research, instruction, and administration. The new CSC consolidated the various components of the Center for Health Sciences. The center, established in 1970, incorporated the schools of Medicine, Nursing, Pharmacy, and Allied Health Professions, along with the various clinical, research, and support services associated with the University Hospital and the health sciences. The new building provided space for the UW Hospital and Clinics, replacing the facilities that had been previously contained in the Wisconsin General Hospital on University Avenue. The complex also included space for the School of Nursing and the Clinical Cancer Center. In many ways, the new facility with its modular structure symbolized the contemporary university. It was multifaceted and interdependent.

The Waisman Center, located just north and west of the CSC, provided quarters for programs dedicated to the study of mental retardation. It was named after UW professor Harry A. Waisman, who had done pioneering research in testing babies for phenylketonuria (PKU), an enzyme deficiency which produces mental retardation. The Wisconsin Alumni Research Foundation office building, housing administrative headquarters for WARF and for several UW units and programs, further enhanced development on the far western edge of the campus.

Substantial growth continued south of University Avenue, with the addition of Weeks Hall for geology and geophysics and the Geology Museum, the Kurt Wendt Engineering

Library, Noland Hall for zoology, and two major centers for instruction and research in education—the Educational Sciences and Teacher Education buildings.

Union South came as a response to enrollment increases and a shifting of the campus population distribution. Constructed as an extension of the Memorial Union at the corner of Randall Avenue and Johnson Street, the new building offered dining and recreational facilities and meeting rooms for students, faculty, and staff in the western and southwestern campus area.

The continuing building boom also affected the eastern edge of the campus. Vilas Communication Hall provided facilities for the School of Journalism, communication arts, theater and drama (including two new theaters), and a new headquarters for WHA radio and television. The Elvehjem Museum of Art created gallery space for the university's growing art collection along with offices for the art history department and quarters for the Kohler Art Library.

The decade proved a lively and successful one for Wisconsin athletics. Momentum began to build in 1969 as Wisconsin sports legend Elroy ("Crazylegs") Hirsch returned to serve as athletic director. His enthusiasm and charismatic personality lifted a program which had been in the doldrums to a high plane of achievement. Badger teams began a resurgence, with national championships in hockey and crew and increased strength in football, wrestling, and track.

An important athletic development of the decade was the establishment of a women's intercollegiate program and the appointment of Katherine ("Kit") Saunders as the first women's athletic director. Federal equal rights legislation spurred development of women's athletics, and Wisconsin moved rapidly to institute a comprehensive and competitive program.

This happened as increased television exposure and public demand catapulted intercollegiate sports into the world of big-time entertainment. Athletic prominence influenced other aspects of the university. In some measure, the overall standing or perception of a university was tied to the success of its athletic program, a situation which raised questions about overemphasis. It was not a new concern in the Wisconsin athletic tradition, but it was being acted out on a larger scale, and it involved much higher financial stakes than had previously been the case. It paralleled the substantially expanded development of higher education in the state.

The appointment of Robert M. O'Neil as the third president of the University of Wisconsin System in 1979 marked a watershed. O'Neil became the first president since Clarence Dykstra to have no previous ties to Wisconsin or the university at Madison. In five years vestiges of the previous alignments on the UW System board of regents had gradually withered away. The contours of the educational and political landscape had inalterably changed since 1836, when the Wisconsin Territorial Assembly acknowledged the importance of education in the development of the frontier.

The university had grown so large and complex that it was difficult to capture the scope of its progress as well as its spirit and character in a single narrative. Its present and future would have to be measured more than ever by the sum of its parts.

A Selection of Features from the *Wisconsin State Journal* and the *Capital Times* marking the 125th Anniversary of the University of Wisconsin– MADISON

The university celebrated its 125th anniversary in 1974 with a series of events and publications highlighting its achievements. The observance came as the university and the state universities were merged into a single University of Wisconsin System.

Edwin Young, an economics professor and former dean of the UW College of Letters and Science, returned to the campus in 1968 after a four-year absence serving as president of the University of Maine. Young became chancellor of the Madison campus and in 1977 succeeded John Weaver as president of the UW System. He is seated here in the "President's Chair," a gift of the class of 1901, presented for use on official occasions.

John C. Weaver grew up in Madison, the son of UW speech professor Andrew T. Weaver. After earning his bachelor's and master's degrees, as well as a doctorate in geography, from the university, he went on to serve as a faculty member and administrator at various institutions. He was president of the University of Missouri when the regents named him to be the successor to Fred Harvey Harrington in 1971. A short time after he arrived, Weaver became president of the newly created University of Wisconsin System. He is pictured here showing off a new pair of socks to an obviously appreciative Bucky Badger.

The merger act produced a new alignment and consolidation of public higher education in Wisconsin. This woodcut by Raymond Gloeckler, a member of the UW art faculty, shows a sampling of the complex administrative matters that faced the UW System regents in the early days of merger.

Bascom Hall became the administrative headquarters for the University of Wisconsin–Madison, while the top floors of Van Hise Hall, looming in the background, housed the offices of the UW System president and the board of regents.

Chemist Irving Shain (right), was named to succeed Edwin Young as chancellor in 1977. Shain, who had been a faculty member since 1952 and had served as vice chancellor from 1970 to 1975, returned to the campus after serving as provost of the University of Washington for two years.

The international prominence and quality of the UW faculty was reinforced in 1975 when

Howard Temin, a professor of oncology, received the Nobel Prize for medicine.

The intense antiwar activity of the 1960s dissipated as the 1970s progressed. Nude streakers momentarily replaced the protesters on Bascom Hill.

Later, Wisconsin Student Association president Leon Varjian led a movement to replace polemics with zaniness in student government.

Varjian and his friends pro-
duced such memorable icons as
the Statue of Liberty emerging
from the Lake Mendota ice and
a flock of plastic flamingos
camped on Bascom Hill.

During the 1970s, the inter-collegiate athletic program expanded with the addition of a women's program and new sports such as soccer.

In the late 1970s the city closed off the entire length of State Street and made the blocks between Lake and Park streets into a pedestrian mall. The nearby Hagenah Fountain on the Library Mall provided a periodic source of diversion for children and other occasional water sports enthusiasts.

*This forest of bicycles parked
outside the Memorial Union
symbolizes the dramatic growth
in enrollment through the 1970s
(it surpassed forty thousand by
the end of the decade). The
Union continued to be a major
focus for student and cultural
activity fifty years after its
opening.*

Symbols
and
Mascots

Concurrent with the founding of the university, its leaders felt the need for a sign or symbol that would give the institution a simple and distinctive identity, an image to serve as the official corporate seal. The impulse was natural. As scholar Charles Boutell noted, writing in *Heraldry in America* (1909): "From the very earliest periods, we find it to have been an usage universally prevalent amongst mankind for both individuals and communities to be distinguished by some *Sign, Device* or *Cognizance*."

At their inaugural meeting in October 1848, the regents formed a committee to develop a seal. In the interim, beginning in 1850, they used the eagle side of the United States half-dollar. While properly patriotic, the eagle offered no logical association with Wisconsin or the university.

In addition to his other assignments, involved primarily with establishing the university on a firm institutional and academic footing, Chancellor John H. Lathrop was instructed to come up with an appropriate corporate device. Governor Nelson Dewey also asked Lathrop to suggest a seal for the state of Wisconsin. While no record remains of what he suggested for the state, his proposal for the university seal does survive.

In February 1854, just five years after the first classes were held and a few months before the first commencement, Lathrop wrote the following memo which was endorsed by the regents:

February 11, 1854

To the Board of Regents,

The undersigned was instructed, at a former meeting of the Board, to procure a seal with suitable device, for their corporate use. After consultation with members of the Board and others, the following simple device was decided upon:

The human eye, upturned to receive the light falling upon it from above; the motto in illuminated letters above the eye, "Numen Lumen," (God our light); the legend around the rim of the seal, "Universitatis Wisconsinensis Sigillum."

The work was executed in Cincinnati, under written instructions, which were not very strictly observed, and justice is not in all respects done to the design. I regard the seal, however, as on the whole a good one, and recommend its adoption by the board.

Respectfully submitted,

J. H. Lathrop

The specific correlation between the elements in Lathrop's design and the university has never been satisfactorily established. Nevertheless, it is interesting to note that the eye with the radiant beams is a part of the "Eye of Providence" design which appears on the reverse side of the Great Seal of the United States. The same design also is pictured on the reverse side of the dollar bill.

The source of the motto *Numen Lumen* and its intended meaning have been matters of considerable speculation and sometimes controversy since the motto first appeared. Much of this speculation occurred because Lathrop's letter was lost in the files until Curti and Carstensen initiated research in preparing their history of the university.

Lathrop had translated the Latin motto as "God our light"—light in this instance presumably signifying divine inspiration. The first attempt to elaborate on his original intention can be traced to James D. Butler, who died in 1905 after serving nearly fifty years as a faculty member and chaplain of the state senate. Butler claimed that Chancellor Lathrop, a Greek and Latin scholar, had likely taken the motto from a British military man who had gained distinction in the seventeenth century as a moderating influence in the struggles between England and Scotland. The motto of the first earl of Balcarres (1618–1659) was *Astra Castra, Numen Lumen*, or, as Butler translated it, "Stars my camp; God my light." Butler claimed that Lathrop appropriated the latter part of the motto and used it for the university in keeping with the religious tone that pervaded many universities at the time.

In 1912 Herbert Barrows Lathrop, a professor of English literature, gave additional resonance to the interpretation in an article which appeared, as did Butler's, in the *Wisconsin Alumni Magazine*. Professor Lathrop noted that several biblical passages used *lumen*, or light, "in a figurative sense, to mean the intellect."

"The symbolism of the eye," Lathrop said, citing the work of Latin scholars, "is used for the faculty of seeing, and is applied to the mind." After plunging deeper, to more arcane associations of the motto with such writers as Isaac Watts, John Milton, and Victor Hugo, and after comparing the motto with similar ones from other universities, Professor Lathrop concluded, "The real meaning of numen is made perfectly clear by the eye and rays. If in classical Latin numen means a divine power manifested in any way, and if intellectual light comes from every direction to man provided he looks up, then to the believer in one God, the numen which is light should mean the power of God manifest throughout the universe. . . . Numen lumen, then, is: 'The divine within the Universe, however manifested, is my light.'"

Professor Lathrop's somewhat ponderous translation did not capture anyone's imagination sufficiently to supplant Chancellor Lathrop's version. "God our light" has come to be accepted as the orthodox translation.

In addition to a variety of semantic interpretations, Chancellor Lathrop's seal has undergone several graphic transformations since it first appeared. These changes seem motivated by efforts to provide a "contemporary" version that speaks to new generations conditioned by a changing visual environment, to create an image that goes beyond the "simple device" advanced by Lathrop. Even though tastes and styles have changed, a certain classical purity about the original design transcends the fashions of the moment, giving it an enduring quality.

The merger of the University of Wisconsin and the Wisconsin state universities necessitated a basic modification of the seal in the 1970s. The merger act dissolved the former corporate identity of the University of Wisconsin and created the University of Wisconsin System in its place. The Latin *Universitatis Wisconsinensis Sigillum* which encircled the original design was consequently modified by inserting "University of Wisconsin–Madison" to represent the change. In 1975, near the close of the university's one hundred twenty-fifth anniversary observance, a campus-wide contest was initiated to develop a new version of the seal. Professor Philip Hamilton of the art department executed the design chosen. It featured a highly modern, hard-edged stylization of the eye and rays surrounded by the legend "University of Wisconsin–Madison."

The seal of the UW System provides much more direct associations with Wisconsin. It features a map of the state pinpointed with the locations of the various components of the system and commemorates significant dates in the development of the University of Wisconsin and the establishment of the system.

The same impulse that led to the preparation of the university seal certainly guided the development of a university mascot. The badger had a familiar state association. The connection came from the lead miners who worked the deposits in southwestern Wisconsin during the 1820s and 1830s. The miners used to burrow, like badgers, into the hillsides as they dug caves to provide shelter from the cold weather. The badger appears on the crest of the state seal adopted in 1851. But even though the image of the badger evoked the state of Wisconsin even before the state was formally established, the legislature did not officially adopt the badger as the state animal until 1957. Even then, the badger had to share billing with the white-tailed deer, the official state wildlife animal.

The connection between the university and the badger first appeared in January 1882, when a student newspaper, the *Campus*, was rechristened the *Badger*. The primary reason for the name change was a desire for uniqueness. "We have selected the new name," the editors explained, "as being appropriate and one which is possessed by no other college publication."

The *Badger* as the name of the student newspaper subsequently was modified when the paper was forced to merge with the *Wisconsin Press*. The resulting publication folded when the *Daily Cardinal* was founded in 1892 and designated as the official paper of the university in 1894 by the faculty.

The next use of the badger appears in 1885, with the publication of *Trochos*, the first university yearbook. The name of this fledgling publication was a Greek equivalent of the word *badger*. The title was anglicized in 1889, when the yearbook became the *Badger*.

A university mascot began to appear in the annals as the intercollegiate athletics program grew. It came to represent a means of defending the university's honor on the playing fields of the Midwest. Early references to a tiger are found in a college yell which appears in the *Badger* yearbook at the turn of the century. Unfortunately, the tiger pictured in most cases looks more like a pussycat than a ferocious jungle beast. An even less intimidating Varsity mascot—a squirrel—surfaced in the 1909 *Badger*.

Only in the second decade of the century did references to badgers appear regularly in accounts of intercollegiate sports. Earlier athletic accounts were punctuated by references to the cardinal, drawing attention to the familiar Wisconsin red worn by the team. About this time efforts to establish a distinctive Wisconsin identity received a considerable boost with the 1909 publication of the university's fight song, "On, Wisconsin." The international popularity of the song, combined with the development of the Wisconsin Idea at about the same time, helped establish a distinctive university identity that has prevailed ever since.

The badger, noted for its particular tenacity and belligerence, began to appear regularly at Wisconsin football games. A wild badger was displayed in a cage on the sidelines at home games, a custom which continued until 1947. Literal depictions of the low-slung badger served as the symbol for Wisconsin teams throughout most of the first half of the century. In 1946, when many Wisconsin athletes had returned to the campus following World War II service, sports publicist Art Lentz saw an opportunity to revitalize interest in Wisconsin sports, particularly football. Lentz, with the assistance of UW artist William C. Shafer, Jr., got the badger "up off his belly" and onto his hind feet. The result was a badger with a sweater carrying a football. This emblem decorated the news releases from the Sports News Service. Similar drawings appeared in many contexts, including the *Badger* yearbook and Homecoming buttons.

Actually, the badger had been up on two feet since 1940. At that time, a California decal manufacturer, the Anson W. Thompson Company of Los Angeles, provided a sheet of decals in response to an order from Brown's Book Store in Madison. The designs, done by artist Arthur C. Evans, featured a belligerent badger wearing a *W* sweater, with his chest thrust outward and his arms raised aggressively as he moved forward in a no-nonsense stride. A scowl wrinkled his brow, and his lips were turned down in an expression of determination. This design has become the standard over the years.

The badger became even more humanized in 1949, when a Wisconsin cheerleader, Bill Sagal, a senior from Sheboygan, put on a papier-mâché badger head, constructed by art student Carolyn ("Connie") Conrad. Sagal augmented his outfit with a pair of boxing gloves to go with his regular cheerleading uniform and appeared at that year's Homecoming rally held on the Memorial Union steps. This transformation had been part of a campaign initiated that fall by the student Pep Committee under the leadership of Bill Sachse (also a senior from Sheboygan) to generate enthusiasm for the football team and its new coach, Ivan Williamson.

Along with creating a badger that could lead cheers, the committee sought a name for the university's athletic mascot, asking student organizations to submit suggestions. Alliteration abounded; students advanced such names as Buster, Buddy, Bernie, and Bouncey, but none seemed to fit quite properly. The Pep Committee therefore made an administrative decision and invested their new creation with the regal name of Buckingham U. Badger, or "Bucky" for short. The Buckingham apparently was derived from

England's Buckingham Palace, which was in the news at the time because of the preparations for the Festival of Britain celebration.

Today's sideline Bucky is more sophisticated than the makeshift costume that decorated the prototype. He is usually clad in a red-and-white striped sweater or coat and wears a carefully sculptured head and furlike coverall. His sideline antics have become an essential part of the pageantry and high jinks of a football Saturday, a basketball game, or a hockey match. For many, Bucky Badger personifies the Wisconsin spirit.

Shortly after he arrived in Madison to assume his administrative duties, Chancellor John H. Lathrop was directed by the regents to prepare an official seal for the university. In the interim, the eagle side of a United States half-dollar was designated as the corporate seal, but no record exists showing how—or if—the eagle was actually used on official documents.

The design for the university's first and enduring official seal was executed in Cincinnati and approved by the regents on February 11, 1854. Lathrop never explained the significance of the eye and the converging rays or the origin of the motto Numen Lumen. The meaning of both has been the subject of considerable scholarly speculation over the years.

*This small plaque (2½" × 1⅞")
was executed by V. D. Brenner
and cast in bronze for the 1904
Jubilee commemorating the
fiftieth anniversary of the
university's first graduation.
The casting features the* Numen
Lumen *motto in the upper left
corner. James D. Butler, writing
in the October 1904* Wisconsin
Alumni Magazine, *contended
that "Brenner's artistic motive
or cardinal idea is an ideal of
aspiration and inspiration. In
his handiwork, however, it is
more evident that the torch in
one hand of the climber stands
for* Lumen *than the uplift of the
other hand is in prayer to*
Numen *for more of that
enlightening." No use of the
plaque or its image was made
following the Jubilee.*

*The original university seal has
undergone a number of
transformations and interpretations over the years to reflect
changing graphic styles and
perceptions. The examples here*
*and on pages 303–304 show
interesting variations on the
specific theme. None of the
variations has supplanted the
original design.*

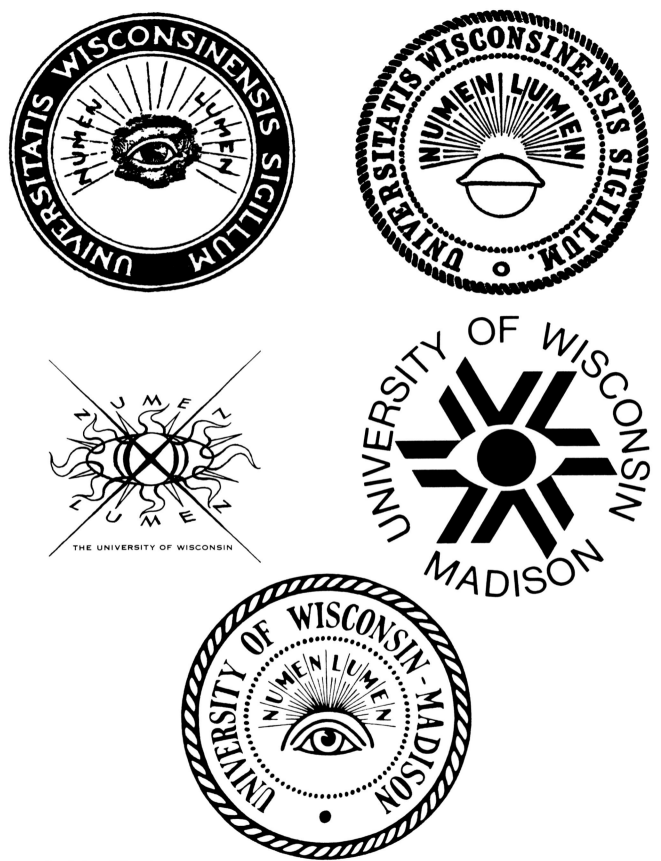

The University of Wisconsin

System

The creation of the University of Wisconsin System through the merger of the University of Wisconsin and the state universities brought a new corporate symbol. The dates on the official seal commemorate the beginning of classroom instruction (1849), the legislative reorganization (1866), and the merger (1971).

The University seal appears regularly on many university documents and publications. It also has been incorporated into the physical design of the campus; the seal appears in the inlay on the second floor of the Memorial Library and the floral pattern in front of Lathrop Hall. The UW or W motif is found in areas such as the front of Agriculture Hall, the south side of the Humanities Building, and the north side of the Field House.

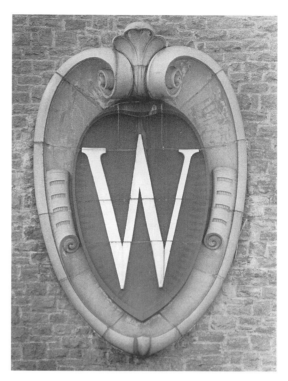

The university's first mascot apparently was a tiger. The use of the tiger, however, was comparatively short-lived, perhaps because the beast never managed to look like anything more than an overgrown pussycat.

U RAH·RAH   WISCONSIN
U RAH·RAH   WISCONSIN
U RAH·RAH   WISCONSIN
                TIGER

A variety of live mascots served as sideline inspiration during Wisconsin football games in the 1920s. These included a black bear, a bonnet monkey, and live badgers. Badgers continued to be the most prominent, and their sideline presence continued well into the 1940s.

In 1949 a human version of the badger mascot appeared at the Homecoming pep rally, replacing the live badger. The new badger received a name which has since become his official moniker—Buckingham U. Badger, or Bucky for short. The individual under the papier-mâché head in this picture is cheerleader Bill Sagal. Football captain Robert J. ("Red") Wilson is in the left foreground.

3-24-48

UNIVERSITY OF
WISCONSIN
SPORTS NEWS SERVICE   ART LENTZ, EDITOR

'11 LANGDON ST.
MADISON 6, WIS

FOR IMMEDIATE RELEASE

In 1946 Art Lentz, head of the Sports News Service, introduced the idea of a rampant badger, off his forelegs and up and running, as a graphic means of stimulating interest in the football team. This rendering, by artist William C. Shafer, Jr., first appeared on athletic news releases.

Over the years the badger likeness has appeared on a variety of novelty items ranging from sweatshirts to swizzle sticks and other promotional items, such as these 1949 Homecoming buttons. The possibilities have been limited only by the ingenuity of the entrepreneurs creating the items for sale.

Although the cartoon version of the badger did not gain wide acceptance until the late 1940s, it actually appeared just before World War II. Arthur C. Evans of the Anson W. Thompson Company in Los Angeles, California, created a set of decals in response to a request from Brown's Book Store in Madison. That set included the drawing of Bucky Badger which has become the standard representation. Other versions were provided for the Student Book Exchange and the University Book Store.

Historic Traditions

Compiled by Anne Biebel

The University of Wisconsin, with the exception of the perennial fascination students had for dunking one another in the lake, had no distinctive student traditions or customs until the early twentieth century, when the student body rather self-consciously created some. In the style of British "fagging," the freshmen were put at the mercy of the sophomores, who dutifully enforced a set of rather demeaning and arbitrary rules. The first twenty-five years of this century saw the development of many annual events that rose to the status of tradition among a student body eager for the historic past these seemed to imply.

Beginning in the 1920s disinterest caused a marked decrease in enthusiasm for carrying out the traditions established by the students of the preceding two decades. Since that time student traditions have come and gone with the particular makeup of the various student generations and in response to the changing scene beyond the campus. Many of the traditions that prevail have fraternities and sororities as their instigators or university athletic events as their focus. The body-passing at Camp Randall on football Saturdays in the 1980s was a comparatively mild form of student diversion when one considers the unleashed rowdyism of student-sponsored events of the early twentieth century.

Another tradition, a rather common one perhaps, is the practice of recording tradition. The material presented here is drawn from many sources, including Curti and Carstensen's *The University of Wisconsin: A History, 1848–1925*; Robert Gard's *University Madison U.S.A.*; the recent UW Band history *Songs to Thee, Wisconsin*; the *Wisconsin Alumnus* magazine; the *Daily Cardinal*; the *Badger*; and assorted histories and other records.

Indian Burial Mounds

Charles E. Brown, curator of the museum of the State Histor-
ical Society from 1908 to 1943, wrote extensively on the tradition of mound-building. His
descriptions remain important to the study of the Indian culture of this region. Brown
promoted the thesis that the earlier mound-builders were the ancestors of the Indians
living in the area at the time of European exploration. Brown described the mounds of the
UW campus in 1914:

In no region in the state are there to be found so great a number of ancient Indian earthworks as in that about the three lakes surrounding the city of Madison.
Every attractive point or sweep of shoreline about these beautiful bodies of water
is or was once the site of a group of mounds. Six of these groups, all of them near
the shore of Lake Mendota, were located on land now owned by the University of
Wisconsin. The classes of mounds represented in the Madison groups are the conical or burial, the linear or wall shaped, and the effigy or emblematic. Represented
among the number of mounds built as effigy types are animal shaped structures
intended to represent the eagle, goose, bear, panther, fox or wolf, and turtle.
Nearly every effigy type found in the southern half of the state is represented by
one or more examples in the Madison area.

According to the late Dr. Reuben Gold Thwaites an effigy mound was at one
time located at the head of the upper campus where University Hall now stands. It
was destroyed when this building was added to the University plant in 1858. It is
said to have been an effigy of the common and widely distributed "panther" type.
Mr. I. N. Stewart states that two mounds, linear in form, were located between
North Hall and the lake bank.

On the crest of Observatory hill are preserved two effigy mounds. They are located at the western extremity of this ridge and within a short distance of Washburn Observatory. One of the mounds is the effigy of a bird. Its wings are spread
and it is represented as flying towards the south. The other effigy, which lies but a
few feet west of the bird mound, represents a turtle but differs from other turtle
effigies in having two converging instead of one central caudal appendage. In this
remarkable mound, the reptile is represented in the act of crawling over the ridge.

Brown also plotted and described the groups of conical and linear mounds found at
Eagle Heights and along the lakeshore to Picnic Point. According to a recent survey that

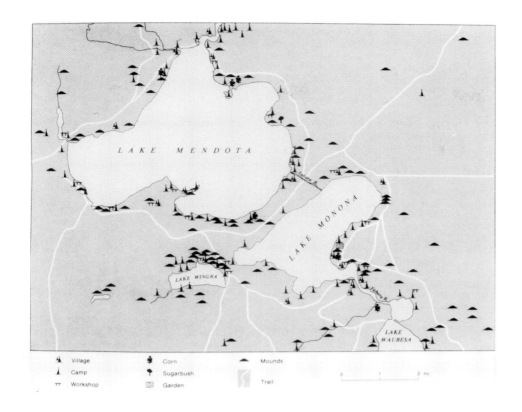

🏕	Village	🌲	Corn	◭	Mounds	
🏕	Camp	🌳	Sugarbush			
⊓	Workshop	▦	Garden		Trail	

0   1   2 mi.

includes the arboretum, there are currently two panther, three bird, one turtle, eighteen linear, and nine conical mounds extant on university properties in Madison.

Names of the Four Lakes

The Winnebago numbered the Madison lakes differently than we do; they began at the north and called our fourth lake first, and so on through the series. Their names for them are

First (Lake Mendota)	Wonk-sheck-ho-mik-la, The lake where the Indian lies
Second (Lake Monona)	Tchee-ho-bo-kee-xa kay-te-la, Tepee lake
Third (Lake Waubesa)	Sa-hoo cha-te-la, Rushes lake
Fourth (Lake Kegonsa)	Na-sa-koo-cha-te-la, Hard-maple grove lake

UNIVERSITY TRADITIONS:

INSTITUTIONAL PRINCIPLES

Tradition of Service to the State: The Wisconsin Idea

Educational service to the state has always been basic to university tradition. Vernon Carstensen, university history professor, explained in the February 1955 issue of the *Daily Cardinal:*

In 1885 the University Regents inaugurated the famous short course in agriculture, which provided for a course consisting of two short winter sessions, to which anyone with a common school education would be admitted.

More important was a legislative bill providing $5,000 for farmers' institutes to be managed by the Regents. The Institutes, which were to be held throughout the state during the winter months, gave the professors a chance to talk to the farmers, and perhaps more important, gave the farmers a chance to talk back.

A veritable agricultural revolution took place, greatly assisted, if not inaugurated by this systematic popular instruction from the university as the center.

By the end of the century the farmers' institutes and other popular educational devices of the College of Agriculture were flourishing. A summer school for science teachers had become so successful that it was incorporated into the regular university program. There was no doubt about it; the university was consciously seeking to use President Thomas C. Chamberlin's words, "a universal educational influence in the community tributary to it," and it had found some successful means of extending that influence.

At this juncture several important events occurred. Robert M. La Follette was elected to the governorship in 1900. A graduate of the university in 1879, he had, by his own statement, been profoundly influenced by President John Bascom, Chamberlin's immediate predecessor. In 1903 Charles R. Van Hise, a university classmate of La Follette's, became president of the university. He, too, had studied under Bascom and had been both student and colleague of Chamberlin.

In his inaugural address Van Hise proposed that professors be used as technical experts by the state government. He felt that professors had knowledge that might be useful in helping to solve various social and political problems. Nor did he propose this in vain. Governor La Follette had already begun to use them in state positions.

In 1912 the legislative reference library listed 46 men who were serving both the university and the state. While it is impossible precisely to measure the influence of the university professors upon legislation and state government, it is clear that some of these men for a time exercised a powerful force. The growth of the university extension continued when the legislature of 1907 passed an appropriation of $20,000 for this work.

Today the "Wisconsin Idea" of public service has grown and expanded to the point where, in the words of the famous slogan, "the boundaries of the campus are the boundaries of the state."

Academic Freedom

The plaque affixed to the front of Bascom Hall declares what has come to be regarded as the university's traditional credo of academic freedom. It reads:

Whatever may be the limitations which trammel inquiry elsewhere, we believe that the great state University of Wisconsin should ever encourage that continual and fearless sifting and winnowing by which alone the truth can be found.

This statement was excerpted from a board of regents report, dated September 18, 1894, that was issued at the conclusion of a hearing at which Richard T. Ely, university economics professor, was exonerated from charges of acting out Socialist sympathies. The superintendent of public instruction, Oliver E. Wells, had accused Ely of promoting unionism and provoking strikes in Madison. After several meetings of the board, at which public support was clearly with Ely, the regents issued a decision that concluded with the now-famous remark. According to a statement made by Richard Ely, the author of the report was university president Charles Kendall Adams.

In 1910 academic freedom had resurfaced as a campus issue, so the use of this statement had particular relevance. That spring, anarchist Emma Goldman's Madison speaking engagement and her association with economics professor E. A. Ross had generated quite a bit of controversy. The board of regents issued a formal resolution censuring Ross for his purported endorsement of Goldman's political views.

At the urging of *La Follette's Magazine* editor Fred MacKenzie, the plaque was cast in bronze by the class of 1910 as its commencement gift to the university. The regents did not particularly welcome the plaque. Its timeliness and promotion by a liberal element caused disdain among the regents, who were growing increasingly conservative with changes in state government.

For five years the plaque was relegated to the basement of University Hall. The class of 1910 rallied and began a campaign to have the plaque dedicated at their five-year reunion. The campaign, which involved the lobbying of regents and the manufacture of streetcar posters, was eventually successful.

At the dedication of the plaque on July 15, 1915, Van Hise commented, "The principles of academic freedom have never found expression in language so beautiful, words so impressive, phrases so inspiring. It was 21 years ago that these words were incorporated in a report of the Board of Regents exonerating a professor from the charge of 'Socialism' that was brought against him. . . . And from that day to this, no responsible party or no responsible authority has ever succeeded in restricting freedom of research and teaching within these walls."

STUDENT TRADITIONS AT
THE UNIVERSITY OF WISCONSIN

Earlier in the twentieth century, the term *tradition* implied, not an event customary to the university population, but instead the code by which the freshmen were to conduct themselves. "Traditions" were established at the university by the class of 1905, and the following rules were put into effect:

1. No freshman shall smoke a pipe or be seen to carry a pipe when on the street or outdoors within the city of Madison.
2. No freshman shall carry a cane or walking stick at any time, unless such cane

1910 now kneel and listen
To the oracle of men!
Fate declares that you are worthless
Death awaits you, 1910

Freshies fly back to your fathers,
Run you rowdy rumdum mokes,
Execration foul and filthy,
Sizzles as old satan stokes,
Hot and hotter grows his hot-house,
Mean and meaner is his mien,
Evil egg-bespattered freshmen,
Num skulls never were so green.

Mushheads, mickies, mammas' tootsies,
Uncouth, ugly, useless he's,
Senseless, soaks, so sad and sloppy,
Turn your tails; take to the trees!

Direful doom o'erhangs dull dunces
In Mendota's icy brine;
Each and every brainless freshy
Will be drowned by **1909**

or stick is necessary because of injuries making it impossible for him to walk without the aid of such a cane or stick.

3. No freshman shall wear any derby or stiff hat during the year until May 1, save only upon "prom" night.

4. No freshman or sophomore shall under any circumstances whatever sit upon the fence in front of the red gym. This rule applies to all freshmen and sophomores without exception.

These rules were presented in the November 1904 issue of the *Wisconsin Alumnus,* which went on to comment, "Members of the class of 1905 were conscious, as have been many seniors before them, of the absence at the University of any distinctive class customs, such as are particularly characteristic of eastern college life. . . . the worthy seniors fell into an ancient error in thinking that these interesting customs and rules needed only to be transplanted to flourish at Wisconsin. . . . That such a fundamental error as to the nature of college traditions should be made by practically an entire student body is surprising."

In May 1909 the "traditions" added regulations insisting that freshmen wear green caps except in the winter months and denying them the right of wearing corduroy trousers. Also, freshmen were banished from loitering or sitting on the steps of the State Historical Library. That "the frosh must obey or be tossed in the lake" was an oft-repeated phrase on the campus until October 19, 1909, when the administration decreed that all hazing (particularly those activities involving the lake) end immediately.

STUDENT EVENTS AS TRADITIONS AT
THE UNIVERSITY OF WISCONSIN

Campus Pump

The campus pump, which stood in the center of the upper campus in front of old North Hall, furnished one of the earliest university traditions. At this pump, in the 1850s and 1860s, freshmen were held beneath its spout and "baptized." This may have been the place of origin of the lake parties of later years when frightened "frosh" coming down the hill from their classrooms at noon were herded towards the North Park Street pier and tossed into the chilly waters of Lake Mendota by stalwart sophomores. Some were permitted to take off their coats and lay down their books before this ordeal, but not all.

—Charles E. Brown

Lake Parties

The most common form of hazing on the university campus in the late nineteenth century involved the capture of freshmen by sophomores for the purpose of dunking them in the lake. This behavior was based on whim, with no rules governing it. "Lake Parties," as they were called, occurred regularly with one or many victims subjected to assault at any given time. They represent a precursor to the only slightly more structured Lake Rush of the early twentieth century.

Lake Rush

Generally an event scheduled during the fall months, the Lake Rush was a contest between sophomores and freshmen for the possession of a strip of shoreline behind the site of Memorial Union. The contest took place, for the most part, in the water. As part of a larger edict against the practice of hazing, students were forbidden to toss one another into the lake. Issued in the fall of 1909, the ruling banned the Lake Rush but prompted students to design a variation of the contest, the Class Rush.

Class Rush

Instituted in the fall of 1909, the Class Rush continued through the teens as an open unleashing of tensions between the freshmen and sophomore men. Julia Hanks Mailer offers this account:

Then there was the bag rush on the lower campus. It had some "lake" connotations, too. They had large sacks eight or nine feet long, good and broad and stuffed with straw. They lined these sacks up in a row in the middle of the lower campus with freshmen on one side and the sophomores on the other, and when the whistles blew everyone went at it! The object was to get as many sacks as possible back to your home goal. The lower campus was always trampled down from being used for sports events. The sophomores had the upper hand, as they knew what it was all about. The freshmen, who were mostly from upstate Wisconsin, had no idea what they were in for. The sophomores would soak the freshmen side with fire hoses until it was a sea of mud. Then the poor freshmen would slip and slide, plowing through the mud trying to get their trophies across the line. Another trick they had—the freshmen pledges of their fraternities were taken by their own upperclassmen brothers and tied up in the basement so they couldn't get to the rush. Others were taken out into the country and left without their trousers so they couldn't run back into town.

After the bag rush, the winners would parade up State Street. By this time, as you can imagine, their clothes were a mess. They were muddy and their hair tousled. They were singing and yelling. It wasn't a riot though, believe me, it was close to it.

The Freshman Cap

The green cap made its first appearance on the campus in 1901 but did not catch on until several years later. The beanie was made of green felt and sported a pink button at its top. In some years, the caps were emblazoned with the class numerals of the wearer. With the institution of university "traditions," use of the cap became increasingly mandatory. Freshmen were given certain dispensations in 1909, when it was not required that the cap be worn between Thanksgiving and Easter. Apparently the winter of 1908 had been particularly fierce, and several freshmen had suffered frostbitten ears. Spring brought the annual cap-burning ceremony, in which freshmen constructed a huge bonfire on the Lower Campus for the purpose of consuming

the loathsome beanies. This was typically followed by a riotous snake-dance parade up State Street to the capitol.

Panty Raid

An incident that occurred on Halloween night in 1899 was repeated a number of times, in one form or another, during the days of separate living units for men and women. That night, as part of the student-organized Night-Shirt Parade, a large group of male students marched around Madison in their pajamas. As the

Cardinal later reported, this group was joined by a "rough set of city hoodlums" as they were making their way to Chadbourne Hall to serenade the women. Once at Chadbourne, things got out of hand. Several rogues stole into the Chadbourne laundry and made off with an assortment of women's underthings, decorated themselves with the plunder, and continued their torchlit parade. In the late 1950s the tradition was briefly revived with variation. Instead of visiting with song, the young men of the campus paid visits to the women's residences with pails of water. Within the context of the waterfight that typically ensued, the young women of this era surrendered their underthings through open windows, accompanied by torrents of water.

Lincoln Statue

The solemn bronze Lincoln that casts his gaze toward the state capitol was placed on Bascom Hill in 1909. It is the single duplicate of an original that was cast in 1906 by New York artist Adolph Alexander Weinman, intended for the town of Lincoln's birth, Hodgenville, Kentucky. When it became known that a single replica of the statue was to be cast, Weinman received several substantial bids. Richard Lloyd Jones (a cousin of Frank Lloyd Wright), who had been involved with the restoration of the Lincoln birthplace, secured the replica for the university. Thomas Brittingham, Sr., provided for the shipping of the piece and the construction of its pedestal. The exedra, completed ten years later, is based on plans by Weinman.

Skyrocket

A skyrocket refers to the greeting given by appreciative students to their favorite professors. The verbal equivalent of the actual shooting-off of a skyrocket, it began with a long hiss, followed by a resounding boom-a-h-h-h, after which the professor's name was shouted amid happy whistles. This tradition enjoyed certain longevity on the campus, beginning just after the turn of the century and continuing into the 1950s. A professor's popularity could be easily gauged by the exuberance and the regularity of the skyrockets he or she received in the course of the semester.

Venetian Night

Venetian Night was a late spring celebration that featured water competitions during the day such as swimming, diving, and canoe-tilting. At night the entire waterfront was lit with decorated floats and illuminated piers. The finale brought a large fireworks display.

Venetian Night was instituted in the first decade of the twentieth century, reaching the pinnacle of its grandeur in the teens. Poor weather caused the event to be canceled for a number of years, though it enjoyed a short-lived comeback in the 1920s.

May Fete

May Fete was an annual spring event, sometimes associated with Venetian Night and sometimes with commencement. It was at its height of popularity during the teens, though it continued into the 1920s. May Fete consisted of processions and dances performed by costumed women students on Bascom Hill. The performance was intended to celebrate spring, the program often consisting of dances to honor lake and forest spirits, along with choreographed celebrations of spring flowers. A maypole, adorned with ribbons and blossoms, stood by throughout, to be used in a maypole dance, which was typically the culmination of the event.

This excerpt from the 1936 *Badger* yearbook gives a sampling of the variety of activities that once surrounded commencement:

> With graduation came a series of events which have faded almost completely out of the University's picture.
>
> The *Ivy* which climbs North Hall, the first of the University buildings (plantings later took place around Bascom Hall), was annually added by a selected orator of the senior class, who presented the *Ivy Oration* in behalf of his classmates. This was usually followed by the *Tombstone Ceremony*, in which the class dedicated its contribution to the stone monuments along Muir Knoll. Both of these customs have passed in a day of scientific landscaping and senior gifts to the student loan funds.

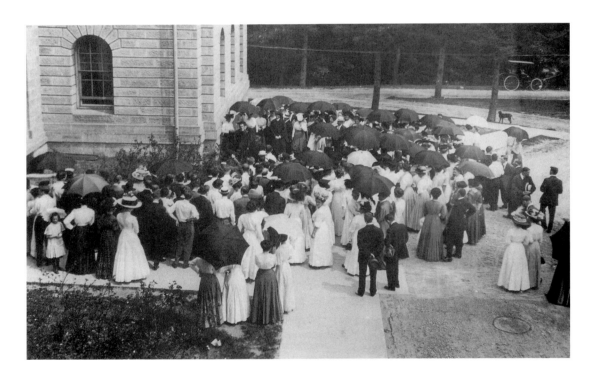

> *Senior Swing-Out*, in which the senior women bid the University good-bye and in which women's honoraries are announced, has been held here for years past, and at present is the last of the big upper campus pageants which remains.
>
> In Commencement week, and theoretically on the night before graduation, senior men have what is the equivalent of Swing-Out. The *Pipe of Peace ceremony*, which once included eight or ten of the outstanding men of the class and a representative of the junior class, has become what is practically a burlesque on all

other senior ceremonials, but the chief purpose of the event—that of getting another silk ribbon sewed onto the stem of the old calumet—is still achieved.

Commencement itself has been held in so many places and under such varying
conditions that to many older alumni and townspeople it still seems strange that it
should always be in the field-house. Many years ago they were held in Music Hall,
and since then they have moved to the stock pavilion, the stadium, and the field-
house.

Varsity Welcome

When the freshman of the early 1920s came to Madison, no elaborate Orientation week was planned out to help him in becoming accustomed to the ways in which the university does things. Instead, he joined thousands of other freshmen and upper classmen in the Varsity Welcome on the upper campus. A colorful parade up the hill served to introduce him to some of the men who took important places in his life.

—1936 Badger

In front of Bascom Hall, the group gathered before a rostrum at which different distinguished members of the university faculty and administration offered comments to assist in the orientation of new and returning students. The event served as something of an academic pep talk and was scheduled during the first days of the fall semester.

Union Vodvil

Union Vodvil, sponsored by the Men's Union, was a highlight of the year mainly because of the students taking part in it. It usually attracted the best talent from all of the dramatic clubs, and such stars as Chubby Goodlad and "Port" Butts, as well as Heinz Rubel and Chic Sale, starred in skits or individual acts. Almost annually a sorority chorus would place well up in the rankings.

The Vodvil skits were usually quite short and rather simple, with Topsy-and-Eva acts rather typical of the general level of entertainment, but often cowboy bands or tabloid minstrel shows would be entered.

—1936 Badger

Vodvil waned by the mid-1920s, as the Haresfoot dramatic organization came to increased prominence on campus. Though Haresfoot and Union Vodvil had roughly simultaneous development and different organizational purposes, most cite Vodvil as the precursor or parent organization of Haresfoot.

Haresfoot

Haresfoot Drama club, its name inspired by the oldtime make-up applicator, was founded by Ernst H. Kronshage in 1898. The first production, Dumas' *Edmund Kean* took place in Madison on February 14 of that year. For the first eleven years the club had a mixed membership that presented heavy drama. In 1909, however, the club was granted a state charter and, with that act barred women and coined the now famous slogan, All our girls are men, yet every one's a lady.

—*The Badger Quarterly*, December 1947

Haresfoot productions traveled throughout the country and enjoyed great popularity in the state. Membership in the club was considered an honor, and many students attempted to join, though it often meant donning feminine attire and affecting womanly mannerisms. Haresfoot, because of overexpenditure on the 1927 production *Ivan Ho,* was in financial distress from that year through the Depression. When revived, productions were less seriously conceived, with drama taking a second place to the humorous effects of football players in women's clothing.

Prom

Prom began before the turn of the century as a trip to Middleton during a hectic week of house parties. In the 1910 era the Prom was held at the then new Armory, and the collegians of that day attempted such steps as the schottische on the bare basketball court. The State Capitol was the next home of the Promenaders and the Proms of the roaring twenties had all of the trappings of a royal ball. With the opening of Memorial Union in 1928, Prom came back to campus. It has been held in the Great Hall almost every year since, and is rivaled in spectacle only by the Military Ball.

—*Daily Cardinal*, Registration Issue, February 1955

Homecoming

Homecoming activities, including fraternity and sorority decoration, are almost as old as football. With the huge bonfires and mass meetings still included among the traditions the University celebrates, it seems strange that some of the others should have died out along the way. Even now, crowds of 6,000 for the Friday night rally are not unknown, and the inexplicable winning tradition that goes with Homecoming is remembered only too well by some of the teams which have opposed Wisconsin teams on that day.

—1936 *Badger*

The first Homecoming celebration took place on November 18, 1911, with over three thousand attending. Buttons urging the team to "Wallop Minnesota" were put on sale, beginning an associate tradition. At the "monster mass meeting" held in the Red Gym on

1955 HOMECOMING QUEEN

the night preceding the game, Coach John Richards told the team and its supporters that football was "emerging from the middle ages into Renaissance light." Throughout the festivities, men and women were segregated, an aspect of the tradition that has obviously passed into oblivion.

St. Patrick's Day

The engineers, celebrating the undoubted fact that "St. Patrick was an Engineer," annually hold their St. Pat's day parade, which is staged on almost any day but St. Patrick's. Almost as traditional is the barrage of eggs which they face, supposedly from lawyers but more frequently from the host of freshmen which any prospect of a fight brings forth.

—1936 *Badger*

Once St. Patrick's day was a signal for a rotten-egg and tomato free-for-all between the lawyers and engineers. Today a staid engineering exposition is all that remains of the feud, along with a parade at the Homecoming football game each fall in which the lawyers march down the field and toss their canes over the goal post.

—*Daily Cardinal*, Registration Issue, February 1955

The Brown Derby

When I came to Madison in 1912, directly from my internship at the Philadelphia General Hospital, I found that a majority of the students in the classes I taught were at least contemporaries, if not older than I. Accordingly, I had to find some device by which I could fill the gap. I used about every expedient that teachers usually use to get and hold the attention of their students, and finally I thought of one that hadn't been used. In those days there was a saying in the East where I came from . . . and this was before the days of Al Smith. . . . the saying was: "Well that takes the brown derby!"

I began using this slang saying to apply to a student who wasn't answering properly. When he gave it to me wrong I would say to him, "That takes the brown derby!" It seemed to work. At least they got to expect it, and it emphasized the correctness of their answer.

The real beginning of the brown derby tradition was in 1913 when the students that year gave me a brown derby. They thought, I suppose, that if I was going to use the saying there might as well be a hat to go with it. It surely did keep them on their toes. They would anticipate getting the hat, and it became a matter of both humor and real incentive. When occasions arose when the derby was called for, either the student or the instructor would call, "The Hat!" and it would be passed along.

—Dr. William Middleton

Rathskeller Lore

The Rathskeller was first opened on October 4, 1928. Originally it was to be called the Tap Room, the idea for this name coming from the Michigan Union's Tap Room. But when Leon Pescheret, the Memorial Union decorator, saw the room he thought it looked like an old German rathskeller. So he developed it as such. . . .

The Rathskeller paintings were done by Eugene Hausler, a native of Germany who came to this country when he was a young man and who learned his trade in Europe when he was only a small boy. Hausler said, "This is one of the few authentic rathskellers in the country. There used to be lots of them, but prohibition killed them. Seldom do you find any like this one. They have them in almost every University in Germany."

The paintings on the Rathskeller's walls embody the idea of student life. The mural above the east fireplace represents the lighter, merry-making side of college life (the sloth), and the one over the west fireplace shows the serious side (the wise bird). The six decorated spandrels with their inscriptions in German symbolize the six major extracurricular activities of the students. . . .

The Rathskeller took over most of the functions of Dad Morgan's soda fountain and billiard room, which used to be on State Street. Dad Morgan's was the gathering place for University athletes and was strictly a men's hangout. It was a standard practice to take a fraternity rushee to Dad's for a malt if he seemed like a good prospect. . . . Dad donated the stout oak table that used to stand in the center of his room to the Rathskeller. . . . The table top is now mounted at the far end of the Union billiard room.

The question of women in the Rathskeller was a problem for a long time. The fairer of the sexes first invaded the place legally on Saturday, December 12, 1936, at the debut of talking pictures at the Union. During the 1937 Summer Session the Union Board took action to permit women to use the Rathskeller during the summer session.

During the late thirties and early forties the tide began to turn toward allowing women in the Rathskeller. In November, 1939, the student body was interviewed on the question of allowing both sexes to partake of the joys of the Rathskeller on special occasions. At first both the men and women voted "no." The typical reaction of the women was "Men ought to have a place of their own. But we'd like one too." So the "Katskeller," for girls, was installed in a small room near the Rathskeller, but it was never a success. Then the opinion gradually shifted. As of November 25, 1941, the Rathskeller discarded, in part, its "For Men Only" signs. The Union Council voted to permit women to use the room after 2:30 P.M. each day. . . . The early hours were reserved for men. After World War II started, as more and more men left the campus, the females were allowed in the Rathskeller in the mornings also. . . .

There's one other interesting inscription, under the central dome, which generations of Wisconsin students—as well as faculty—can probably remember: "It is the custom here at the Union that he who eats and drinks, also pays for it. Such a guest is a dear and cherished friend, who promptly pays for what he gets."

—Mary Waters, *Wisconsin Alumnus*, February 1953

The Red Wagon

The Little Red Wagon, composed of an antediluvian Ford chassis and a wooden framework, formed the center of many processions. For years, almost every Wisconsin Football team or crew got its send-offs, including a ride to the station with hundreds of students pulling at the ropes attached to the wagon. Recently the wagon was lost for almost ten years, but it turned up for the 1934 football season and will probably be used intermittently for years to come.

—1936 *Badger*

We did have a little red wagon, of course. They used it to pull the team back to the campus from the station after they had won a game. Of course in the old days the team traveled only by train. There would be a couple of cars for the football players and their gear, and behind that a long string of cars with the fans. If the team won an out of town game, thousands and thousands of people assembled, usually at the old Northwestern depot on Williamson Street, to greet them. They would line up the team on the old red wagon and then the crowd would follow up-town and around the Capitol Square and back to the campus. When the old wagon disappeared, they would sometimes bring them back in a fire truck.

—Jack Kramer

The use of the fire truck, after the final disappearance of the red wagon, provides a direct precedent to the contemporary use of the Bucky Wagon, a restored fire truck used to transport Bucky Badger and his entourage of cheerleaders about town and to Camp Randall Stadium on football Saturdays. The 1932 La France fire engine was donated to the university by Mr. and Mrs. Jay J. Normington in the mid-1970s.

Burning the Boat

The little red wagon and the ceremony of burning the boat were symbols associated for many years with the Wisconsin crew. The wagon was first used to carry the shells from lake to lake. Later it was pressed into service to haul the football team to the railroad station when the team left for out of town games.

Before the crew left for the Hudson river meet each year, the ritual of "burning the boat" was solemnly performed. An obsolete shell was set afire on the lake shore to placate the gods of chance and bring luck to the new shell going east.

—*Wisconsin Alumnus*, February 1947

U Rah-Rah-Wisconsin

It was in the baseball game with Northwestern on May 19, 1884, at Madison, that the university yell, the U rah-rah, Wisconsin, three times repeated, was first heard on the home grounds in intercollegiate sports. . . . The yell came into being by general consent and general use without any vote or other formal action by any students or group of students. Like Topsy, it just growed. Its original cadence was not the same as it is today. The eighteen syllables were spoken or shouted from first to last with the exactly even rhythm of a march. The only change of volume or intonation was in a primary accent stressed upon the last syllable of Wisconsin, and a slight secondary accent on the first syllable of that name, so that the yell was most nearly represented in type, as it was correctly printed in

RAH RAH WISCONSIN

BOOK IV.

E. L. KASTLER

ATHLETICS

The Badger of May 22, 1884. This was the fact as long as I was a student at the university. I do not know how or when the change into the present crescendo-accelerando came to pass. *The Badger* printed all four of the yells of the colleges in the baseball league:

Wisconsin: U! RAH! RAH! WIS-CON-SIN!

Beloit: YIP! YIP! YIP! B-E-L-O-I-T!

Racine: RA! RA! RA-CINE!

Northwestern: N.W.U.U.U.

> —Frederic A. Pike, *A Student at Wisconsin Fifty Years Ago* (1935)

"On, Wisconsin"

"On, Wisconsin" was composed in 1909 by Chicago musician William T. Purdy with UW alumnus Carl Beck, who was responsible for the words. Purdy visited Madison on November 11 of that year to introduce the song at a pep rally. It met with instant success. The song was later promoted by a Milwaukee music publisher, and its popularity spread beyond the state. The song has been adapted to the specific needs of over 2,500 schools and universities. A controversy concerning authorship developed in the early 1950s when Purdy's widow, in correspondence with Ray Dvorak, asserted that "On, Wisconsin" was the sole creation of her husband. The controversy eventually died with pervasive sentiment seeming to accept that the song was the result of collaboration between the pair. With words modified by Carl Beck, the state of Wisconsin adopted "On, Wisconsin" as its official state song in 1959.

"Varsity"

The tradition of arm-waving during the singing of "Varsity" originated in 1934. UW Band director Ray Dvorak had first conceived of the idea ten years earlier. As he described it:

> I was assistant to the band director at the University of Illinois at the time. We took the band, all 160 of them, to the University of Pennsylvania for a big game. Penn hadn't lost a game in a couple of years. It was the year that Illinois' Red Grange was coming into fame. We beat Penn, and at the end of the game Penn students sang their Alma Mater as they did only when they were defeated.
>
> Well, at the end of the song they waved their derbies in the air to the words hail, hail, hail and I thought it was pretty striking so I stuck it in my back pocket.

Later, at Wisconsin, one day when President Glenn Frank was speaking, I cued the students beforehand to watch me and wave their hats at the end of Varsity. The song sort of became a toast to the president.

"Varsity" is an adaptation of a 1853 French hymn composed by Charles Gounod. The Latin verse which offers a prayer for the king translates as "O Lord save thou our King George and hear us when we call upon thee." The hymn's transformation into "Varsity Toast" occurred in 1898, when a young music instructor at the university, Henry Dyke Sleeper, worked with the arrangement and composed suitable words. The singing of the song, now known simply as "Varsity," with its associate gesture remains one of the university's most established traditions.

You've Said It All

This composition by Steve Karmen was first played by the UW Band in 1973. It was offered in response to a group of hockey fans who had been calling for the band to perform a polka. The song was immediately recognized as a jingle used to promote beer. Band director Michael Leckrone considered the sing-along that ensued to be an inappropriate form of advertising. He instructed his band to shout, at the appropriate juncture, the words, "When you say WIS-CON-SIN, you've said it all." It caught on. Later that season, when the Badger hockey team captured the NCAA championship, the band signaled the victory with performances of their new anthem all over Boston. With their return, the song earned a wide appeal and has since been a prominent part of the band's repertoire at all university athletic events.

The Fifth Quarter

"The fifth quarter" (the term supplied by the local press) has its origins in the mid-1970s. As was typical of most university bands, the UW Band provided a postgame show intended to entertain the spectators as they were leaving the stadium. By 1977 the band members came to encourage audience participation, particularly with the student section. The interaction has become more and more animated over the years and has evolved into a stadium party that features dancing, music, and boisterous singing for the many thousands who remain after the football games.

Bibliographical
Essay

Because this book is primarily intended as a pictorial record, the author has not cited each specific reference for information in the text and captions. The text, however, is based on primary and secondary sources which have provided a logical superstructure for both the textual and visual material.

The university has been well served by those who have chronicled its overall history and the development of its many parts. The primary and indispensable source for the early years is the exemplary two-volume work *The University of Wisconsin: A History, 1848–1925*, by Merle Curti and Vernon Carstensen (Madison, 1949). This work is admirable because, in addition to providing a rich chronicle of the development of the university, it also offers insight into the history and growth of higher education in America.

Other useful works of this nature are J. F. A. Pyre, *Wisconsin* (New York, 1920); E. B. Fred, ed., *A University Remembers* (Madison, 1969); Robert Gard, *University Madison U.S.A.* (Madison, 1970); Allen G. Bogue and Robert Taylor, eds., *The University of Wisconsin: One Hundred and Twenty-Five Years* (Madison, 1975); *The Jubilee of the University of Wisconsin* (Madison, 1905); Charles McCarthy, *The Wisconsin Idea* (New York, 1912); David Mollenhoff, *Madison: A History of the Formative Years* (Dubuque, 1982); *Perspectives of a University: A Survey of the Campus—Architectural, Historical, Archeological and Memorial Resources and Recommendations for Preservation* (Madison, 1978); Reuben Gold Thwaites, ed., *The University of Wisconsin and Its History and Its Alumni* (Madison, 1900); Elvehjem Art Center, *The University of Wisconsin: 125 Years through the Camera's Eye* (Madison, 1974); and *A Resourceful University: The University of Wisconsin–Madison in Its 125th Year* (Madison, 1975).

Studies with a special focus include Theodore Herfurth, *Sifting and Winnowing: A Chapter in the History of Academic Freedom at the University of Wisconsin* (Madison, 1949); Michael Leckrone, ed., *Songs to Thee, Wisconsin, 100 Years: The University of Wisconsin Bands* (Dallas, 1985); Nancy Sachse, *A Thousand Ages: The University of Wisconsin Arboretum* (Madison, 1965); Gwen Schultz, *The Bucky Badger Story* (Madison, 1981); John Rector Barton, *Rural Artists of Wisconsin* (Madison, 1948); *The Art of Rural Wisconsin (1936–60)* (Madison, 1985); S. W. Bailey, ed., *The History of Geology and Geophysics at the University of Wisconsin–Madison, 1848–1980* (Madison, 1980); Paul F. Clark, *The University of Wisconsin Medical School: A Chronicle, 1848–1948* (Madison, 1967); Barry Teicher and John W. Jenkins, *A History of Housing at the University of Wisconsin* (Madison, 1987); James S. Watrous, *A Century of Capricious Collecting, 1877–1970: From the Gallery in Science Hall to the Elvehjem Museum of Art* (Madison, 1987); Fannie Taylor, *The Wisconsin Union Theater: Fifty Golden Years*, edited by Mollie Buckley (Madison, 1989); and Paul H. Williams and Melissa Marossy, eds., *With One Foot in the Furrow: A History of the Department of Plant Pathology at the University of Wisconsin–Madison* (Dubuque, 1986).

The following personal remembrances, biographies, and autobiographies have provided useful information and perspectives: Robert M. La Follette, *La Follette's Autobiography: A Personal Narrative of Political Experience* (Madison, 1960); Mark H. Ingraham, *From a Wisconsin Soapbox* (Madison, 1979); Diane Johnson, *Edwin Broun Fred: Scientist, Administrator, Gentleman* (Madison, 1974); William H. Kiekhofer, *To Thee, Wisconsin: State and University and Other Public Addresses* (New York, 1950); Lawrence H. Larsen, *The President Wore Spats: A Biography of Glenn Frank* (Madison, 1965); Alexander Meiklejohn, *The Experimental College* (New York, 1971); John Muir, *The Story of My Boyhood and Youth* (Boston, 1913); and George C. Sellery, *Some Ferments at Wisconsin, 1901–1947: Memories and Reflections* (Madison, 1960).

In addition to these specific sources, the general files of the University Archives have been invaluable—as a source both of specific information and of most of the pictorial material that appears in this volume. Specific periodicals and other sources not otherwise cited include *Aegis* (1886–1900); *Trochos* and the *Badger* yearbook; the *Badger Herald*; the *Daily Cardinal*; the Madison *Capital Times*; the *Milwaukee Journal*; the *Wisconsin State Journal*; the *Sphinx* (1899–1902); the *Octopus* (1919–1942, 1946–1953); the *Student Miscellany*; the *University Press* (1870–1887); the *Wisconsin Alumni Magazine* (subsequently the *Wisconsin Alumnus*); the *Wisconsin Country Magazine* (1907–1959); and the *Wisconsin Engineer* (1896–1966).

Finally, many shorter works, reports, and documents were useful but too numerous to cite in a work of this kind. While the individuals responsible must remain anonymous, they have made important contributions to the record of the university's history and achievements.

Picture Credits

The major portion of the photos and other illustrative material used in this volume comes from the files and collections maintained by the University of Wisconsin-Madison Division of Archives. Some illustrations come from outside sources. Wherever possible, sources are credited below, listed by page number.

University of Wisconsin–Madison Division of Archives: iii; 13; 14 (top); 15; 16 (top); 17; 18 (bottom right); 19 (left); 20; 21; 22; 26; 27; 28; 33; 35; 36; 47 (top); 49; 50; 51; 53; 54, (bottom), Wilfred Chase photo; 58 (top); 59 (bottom); 60; 61 (top); 62; 63, Meuer collection; 64 (top); 66; 67; 68; 75, Gallistel collection; 76; 77; 78, Meuer collection; 79 (top), Meuer collection; 79 (bottom), Kamera Kraft; 81 (top), Meuer collection; 81 (bottom); 82 (top), Meuer collection; 82 (bottom); 84 (top); 84 (bottom), Meuer collection; 85; 86 (bottom), Meuer collection; 87; 88 (bottom), Meuer collection; 90 (top); 91; 95 (bottom); 96 (top), Meuer collection; 96 (bottom); 97,

Meuer collection; 98; 100 (bottom); 101; 102 (bottom), Meuer collection; 103 (top), Meuer collection; 103 (bottom); 104 (bottom), Meuer collection; 105, Meuer collection; 106, Meuer collection; 108, Meuer collection; 111 (middle, bottom), Meuer collection; 112, Meuer collection; 114 (top), Meuer collection; 114 (bottom); 115; 116 (top), McKillop photo; 117, Meuer collection; 118; 119 (top), Meuer collection; 119 (bottom); 130; 131; 132, Meuer collection; 133, Meuer collection; 134 (top); 134 (bottom), Meuer collection; 135, Meuer collection; 136 (bottom), Meuer collection; 137 (top), Meuer collection; 138 (top); 139 (bottom), Meuer collection; 140; 141, Meuer

collection; 142, Meuer collection; 143 (bottom), Meuer collection; 144; 145; 146; 149 (bottom); 150 (top); 151 (bottom); 152; 195; 196, U.S. Navy photo; 197; 199; 200 (bottom); 201; 203; 204 (bottom); 205 (bottom); 206 (bottom); 209 (bottom); 211; 212 (top); 213 (bottom); 221; 222 (middle); 224; 226; 228 (top, bottom); 230 (top); 231 (top); 233 (top); 234 (top); 235 (bottom); 236 (bottom); 237 (top); 249; 250 (top); 252 (top); 254; 255 (top); 260 (top); 261 (top); 262; 263 (bottom); 268; 270; 272; 273 (bottom), Carl Stapel photo; 275 (bottom); 276 (bottom); 283; 290 (bottom); 292; 307 (top left), Meuer collection; 307 (bottom); 308 (middle), Meuer collection; 319; 321; 323;

324; 325 (top left); 325 (top right), Meuer collection; 328; 332; 336; 337.

University of Wisconsin–Madison University News and Information Service: 4, Michael Kienitz; 6, Michael Kienitz; 155, Michael Kienitz; 156 (top), Michael Kienitz; 156 (bottom), Norman Lenburg; 157, Michael Kienitz; 158, Michael Kienitz; 159, Michael Kienitz; 162, Michael Kienitz; 163, Michael Kienitz; 165, Michael Kienitz; 166, Michael Kienitz; 168, Michael Kienitz; 170, Michael Kienitz; 175, Michael Kienitz; 176 (top), Michael Kienitz; 178, Michael Kienitz; 179 (top, middle), Michael Kienitz; 180 (top), Michael Kienitz; 181 (bottom left), Michael Kienitz; 186, Michael Kienitz; 175 (top, middle); 285, Norman Lenburg; 291 (top), Norman Lenburg; 307 (top right), Michael Kienitz.

University of Wisconsin Extension Photographic Media Center: 16 (bottom); 52; 64 (bottom); 119 (middle); 148 (bottom); 150 (bottom); 180 (bottom); 198 (bottom); 202; 205 (top); 208, Gary Schulz; 210; 212 (bottom); 213 (top); 214; 222 (bottom); 225 (bottom); 227 (top), Gary Schulz; 227 (bottom); 228 (middle); 229; 231 (bottom); 232; 235 (top); 250 (bottom), Duane Hopp; 253, Gary Schulz; 257; 258 (top); 261 (bottom), Del Brown; 266 (top), Gary Schulz; 266 (bottom); 267 (bottom); 269 (bottom); 284; 287 (top); 306; 325 (bottom); 330.

State Historical Society of Wisconsin Iconographic

Collections: 14 (bottom), WHi(X3)960; 18 (top), WHi(X28)1171; 18 (bottom left), WHi(X3)25516; 19 (right), WHi(X3)41306; 23, WHi(X3)27542; 24 (top), WHi(X31)17434; 24 (bottom), WHi(X32)8764; 25 (left), WHi(X3)5766; 25 (right), WHi(D487)9783; 30, WHi(X3)27543; 31, WHi(X3)41010; 32 (top), WHi(X22)29; 32 (bottom), WHi(X28)3706; 34, WHi(X3)27817; 37 (bottom), WHi(X3)15110; 38 (top), WHi(X3)18013; 38 (bottom), WHi(X3)1498; 46, WHi(X3)21113; 47 (bottom), WHi(X3)18574; 48, WHi(X2)111; 54 (top), WHi(X3)8612; 55 (top), WHi(X3)41014; 56, WHi(X3)15367; 61 (bottom), WHi(X3)2599; 80, WHi(D486)2764; 83, WHi(X3)18453; 86 (top), WHi(X3)41074; 89, WHi(X3)41078; 90 (bottom), WHi(D487)4547; 92, WHi(B84)66; 93 (bottom), WHi(X3)25565; 94 (top), WHi(X3)46205; 94 (bottom), WHi(X28)3719; 95 (top), WHi(X3)8605; 99, WHi(H31)184; 102 (top), WHi(X3)41073; 104 (top), WHi(D487)1024; 109, WHi(X3)31393; 111 (top), WHi(X3)33841; 113 (top), WHi(X3)41071; 139 (top), WHi(D487)10376; 148 (top), WHi(X3)37753; 149 (top), WHi(D487)10180; 200 (top), WHi(X3)35109; 237 (bottom), WHi(V4)215, Richard Vesey photo.

Badger Yearbook: 5; 55 (bottom); 57; 58 (bottom); 59 (top right); 65; 93 (top); 107; 110; 113 (bottom); 120; 137 (bottom); 138 (bottom); 143 (top); 193; 194 (bottom); 198 (top); 204 (top); 206 (top);

207; 209 (top); 222 (top); 223; 230 (bottom); 233 (bottom); 234 (middle, bottom); 236 (top); 238; 251; 252 (bottom); 255 (bottom); 258 (bottom); 259 (top); 260 (bottom); 271; 308 (top, bottom); 309 (bottom); 317; 318; 334.

Daily Cardinal photo: 274.

Collection of Theo. Erickson: 147 (bottom).

Bruce Fritz photo: 179 (bottom).

Copyright © Michael Kienitz: 181 (top); 288; 289.

Milwaukee Journal photo: 151 (top, middle); 225 (top).

David V. Mollenhoff, Madison © 1982, fig. 1.8: 313 (top).

Chuck Patch photo: 291 (bottom); 313 (bottom).

Radlund & Associates, Inc.: 171.

Todd Rosenberg: 184.

James Sowinski photo: 259 (bottom).

The Sphinx: 59 (top left); 100 (top).

Sports Illustrated photo © by Paul J. Bereswill: 185.

University of Wisconsin–Madison Athletic Department: 194 (top); 290 (top).

WHA-TV photo: 263 (top).

Williamsiana Collection, Williams College, Williamstown, Mass.: 29.

Wisconsin Octopus: 116 (bottom); 136 (top).

Wisconsin State Journal photo by Edwin Stein: 250 (middle).

Index